All Stitched Up

Betty Foster and Joy Gammon

All Stitched Up

Weidenfeld and Nicolson
in association with Channel Four Television Company Limited
and Yorkshire Television Limited

Published in Great Britain by
George Weidenfeld & Nicolson Limited
91 Clapham High Street
London SW4 7TA

ISBN 0 297 78693 8 Cased
ISBN 0 297 78694 6 Paperback

Printed in Great Britain by
Butler & Tanner Ltd, Frome and London

CONTENTS

DRESSMAKING

KNITTING

Acknowledgements
Les Gammon (*Technical Drawings*)
Sue Loveridge (*Illustrations*)
Colin Thomas (*Photography*)
Models Patrick Boyce, Helen Lewis,
Mary McNaulty and Mark Scott.

DRESSMAKING

INTRODUCTION BY BETTY FOSTER

Dressmaking is both an exciting hobby and an economic necessity, and yet there are many people who have never tried their hands at the subject.

Some people, like me, were not able to do it at school because of the time-table clashes with the 'academic' options. Some tried dressmaking at school and decided that they did not like the subject, because it was either boring, the clothes didn't fit, or it all took too long to do, and, very significantly, it was only taught to the girls.

When I came into dressmaking (by accident not design) I was astonished to discover that it was not the dull, arty-crafty subject that I had imagined. It was a mixture of engineering (getting the patterns right and knowing how they worked), geography (to find my way around patterns and instructions), an eye for colour, and some manual dexterity that everyone has to a degree. It needed very little drawing skill, and it certainly didn't need maths.

As the years went by, and I became more and more involved, I became increasingly angry that this magical subject had, by and large, fallen by the wayside. Why had we not recognised its potential for both boys and girls, each with different talents to contribute?

Career opportunities have been lost because of the lack of recognition of the subject's content, and its logical learning pattern ... and so Betty Foster started her crusade.

First the subject must produce successful results, and that means pattern knowledge and correct cutting out. It can be imaginatively and excitingly taught (and learnt), without the making up of full-size garments.

An understanding of pattern construction and adaptation automatically introduces an awareness and understanding of fabric choice, and it is quite amazing how the same understanding makes you apply sewing techniques with caution and increased skill.

Your *aim* is to be *successful* with the clothes you make, to enjoy making them, and to realise that this is a pastime where there is always something new to learn.

New machinery, fabrics, sewing aids, trimmings, are happening all the time, and their introduction can completely alter the methods that you are using. Keep an open mind, knowing that we all learn from each other. Often the time-honoured ways of doing something are still the best, but watch out for the new innovations that can make things a lot easier.

Dressmaking at home needs to become dress-manufacture at home, learning from industry how to do things quicker without losing the quality of workmanship that is perhaps the best reason of all for learning how to create fashionable clothes for yourself and your family.

Whether you are a beginner or an old-hand at dressmaking I hope you will find the hints, tips, and advice in this book useful and enjoyable, and that you will have fun making something new, which you can proudly show to friends knowing that you have the subject 'All Stitched Up'.

DRESSMAKING TODAY ...
HOW TO BEGIN

The age at which you start is not important, although it can be a great advantage to begin when you are between eleven and twelve and have a lifetime's opportunity to get it right from the word go.

I teach lots of students who are over sixty plus, so, if you are a late-starter, or just retired and want a good hobby, or even if you have been sewing for years and want to take a fresh look at the subject, *now* is the time to begin.

You do not do this with full-size patterns, spread all over the floor.

If you copy the front, back, and sleeve pattern from Diagram 1 on to 1 cm squared paper, marking it exactly as illustrated, you will have a miniature *master block pattern.*

Make *three* copies, and stick them on to firm cardboard. This is so that you can draw round the edges easily.

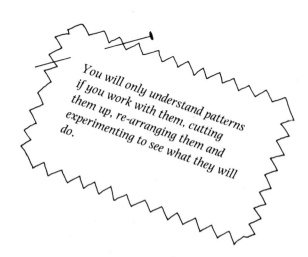

You will only understand patterns if you work with them, cutting them up, re-arranging them and experimenting to see what they will do.

BASIC MASTER PATTERN
Set A
Diagram 1

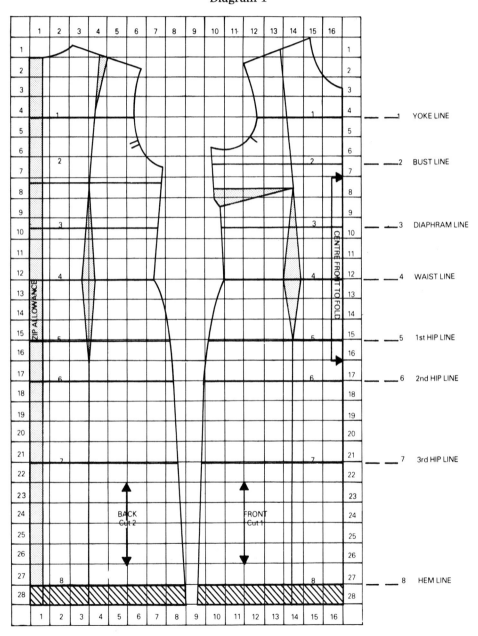

1 YOKE LINE

2 BUST LINE

3 DIAPHRAM LINE

4 WAIST LINE

5 1st HIP LINE

6 2nd HIP LINE

7 3rd HIP LINE

8 HEM LINE

ZIP ALLOWANCE

CENTRE FRONT TO FOLD

BACK
Cut 2

FRONT
Cut 1

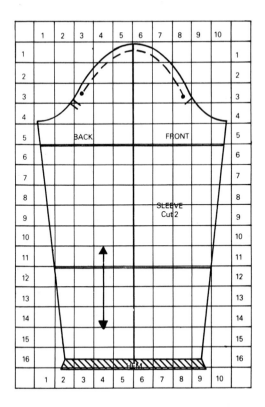

SEAM ALLOWANCES

The diagrams for the miniature patterns include seam allowances of 4 mm, when copied on to 1 cm squared paper.

The centre back seam and hems are as indicated in Diagram 1.

EXPERIMENTING WITH THE PATTERNS
(Set A)

The pattern which has not been cut up will make a simple dress, with set in sleeves, and will depend upon a good choice of fabric, and perhaps the addition of imaginative trimming.

The sleeve can be cut long, three-quarter length, or short.

SLEEVELESS DRESSES

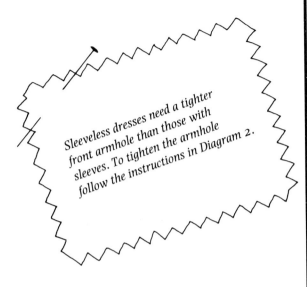

Sleeveless dresses need a tighter front armhole than those with sleeves. To tighten the armhole follow the instructions in Diagram 2.

Tightening to avoid gaping
DIAGRAM 2

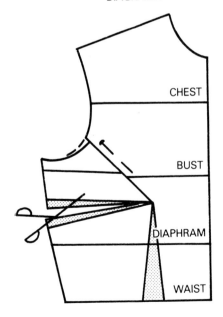

CHEST

BUST

DIAPHRAM

WAIST

LOWER NECKLINES

Before changing the neckline of the Basic Master Pattern you should fold out the back shoulder dart and pin the shoulder seams together. Now draw your new neckline, starting at the centre front and recognising how the shoulder seams and centre back are affected. (Diagram 3)

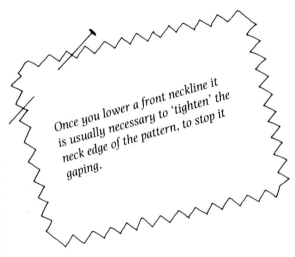

Once you lower a front neckline it is usually necessary to 'tighten' the neck edge of the pattern, to stop it gaping.

Drawing new necklines
DIAGRAM 3

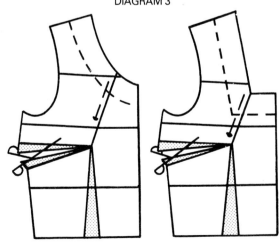

COLLARS

1 Cut out your selected FRONT and BACK neckline.

2 a) Pin the shoulder seams together.

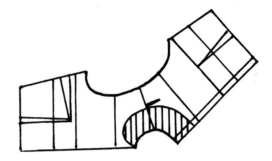

b) Draw in the collar of your choice and make a pattern of it, adding a seam allowance at the outer edge.

c) If the collar is cut from a pattern exactly like this it will be FLAT.

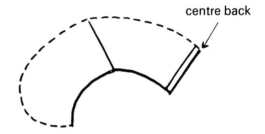

centre back

TO MAKE THE COLLAR 'STAND' CLOSER TO YOUR NECK.

Tighten the outer edge in a series of small darts.

NOTE:

a) This does not alter the neck edge.

b) The collar becomes less curved as you do this.

THE HORIZONTAL JIG SAW PATTERN (Set B)

This pattern has been cut into sections horizontally, and the sleeve has been cut down the middle to form a front and back section. (Diagram 4)

Pattern Set B
DIAGRAM 4

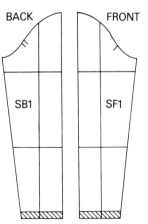

BACK   FRONT

1   YOKE LINE   1

2   BUST LINE   2

3   DIAPHRAM LINE   3

4   WAIST LINE   4

5   5

6   2nd HIP LINE   6

7   7

8   8

HEM LINE

BACK   FRONT

SB1   SF1

USING SET B PATTERNS

Try different combinations of ideas to produce new designs. The ideas can be made either with or without sleeves. The darts, which are sketched at the waistline, are not essential – you can use them to make the garment more fitted to your figure, you can elasticate it, make it into a draw-string waist, or leave the waist darts out altogether and wear it loose. If you decide to keep the waist darts, and then cut through them horizontally, you will have to stitch any parts of darts that are left in the pieces, *before* you stitch the pieces back together again.

The bust dart must be in the pattern somewhere, and, when we use Set C, you will discover how it is used to change the designs. *Use your Set B patterns to try out the ideas from our sketches.*

Designs using horizontal jig saw pattern

SIMPLE DOLMAN, RAGLAN, OR MAGYAR SLEEVES

Using the body patterns from Set A and the sleeve patterns from Set B. Place the front sleeve pattern, and the back sleeve pattern into position as indicated in Diagram 5.

This gives you an entirely new starting pattern, from which you can create raglan and dolman sleeves, dropped shoulder line garments, and cap-sleeve patterns.

Working only with miniature patterns try to make new designs – you will soon get the hang of how the patterns have been made, and you can try out your ideas in scraps of fabric to see that they actually work.

Cutting line for raglan sleeves

DIAGRAM 5

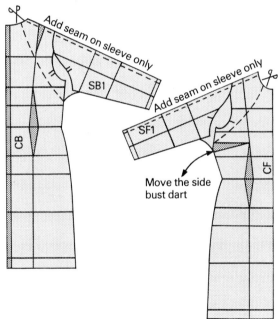

Add seam on sleeve only

SB1

Add seam on sleeve only

SF1

CB

CF

Move the side bust dart

THE 'EXPLODED' PATTERN (Set C)

Preparation

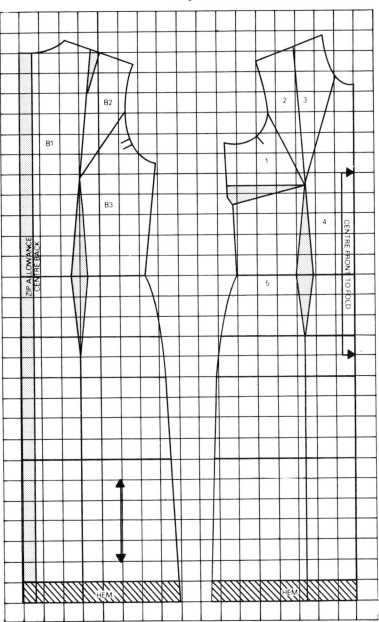

THE 'EXPLODED' PATTERN (Set C)

This pattern has been cut into sections and the darts have been completely cut away.

DIAGRAM 6

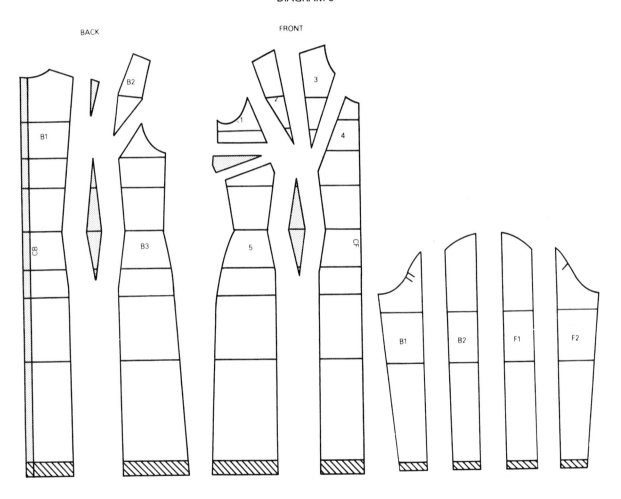

If you re-arrange the sections, for example:

Front Pattern (a) Bring piece 1 to piece 5.
Bring piece 2 to piece 1.

Now

Take piece 3 to piece 4.

you now have the pattern for the princess-line dress, with the long seam containing the shaping of the two darts.
Try it out in fabric.

(b) Bring piece 1 to piece 5.
Take pieces 3 and 2 to piece 4.

You now have the shaped seam, containing the darts, coming from the armhole.

(c) Bring pieces 1, 2 and 3 to piece 5.
Bring piece 4 to piece 5.

You now have a large neckline dart (which can also be gathers).

(d) Bring pieces 2 and 3 together.
Take pieces 1 and 5 to piece 2.
Take piece 4 to piece 3.

You now have a wide flared hem, ideal for a kaftan.

Now try rearranging the back pieces

THE SLEEVES

The sleeve pattern in Set C is cut into four long strips. (Diagram 6)
Try spreading the pattern pieces at the top, whilst keeping the bottom edges together.
Now hold the top together and spread the bottom.

How many styles can you design?

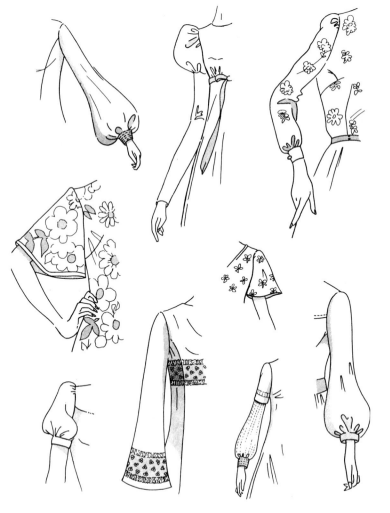

GETTING STARTED

DESIGNING AND ADAPTING YOUR OWN PATTERNS

If you discover that you like working with pattern ideas, and would like to design your own patterns, you should first of all get a copy of my book *Creating Fashion*, which works with your miniature patterns and explains the subject in detail.

You will also have to get a *Master Pattern* of yourself, so that you can copy any of the miniature ideas in *your* size. This is the only way to work if you are *not* one of the so-called standard sizes.

Write to: Betty Foster Ltd, P.O. Box 28, Crewe. CW2 6PH, if you would like further details.

STANDARD SIZE PATTERNS FROM A DIAGRAM

You can *now* copy the diagram pattern on page 10 on to sheets of Betty Foster's Design Paper, which is available in sizes 8, 10, 12, 14, 16, 18, 20, 22, and you will get a Standard Size Master Pattern in the size of paper that you are using. The Design Paper comes in packs of 3 sheets, and can be bought from haberdashery stores, or by post from P.O. Box 28, Crewe CW2 6PH.

BUYING STANDARD SIZE, READY PRINTED, PATTERNS

Understanding patterns in miniature is the best possible training you can have *before* you go to look at the pattern companies' catalogues, because you will totally recognise what is involved, not only in the pattern, but also in the amount of sewing that is needed.

You need to know your size, height, bust, waist and biggest hip measurement.

Buy dress and blouse and coat patterns by your *bust* size (hips are easier to adjust).

Buy skirt and trouser patterns by *hip* size (waists are easier to adjust).

The pattern books contain patterns for different heights, and you should look at this carefully, buying only within your height range, because the patterns are in better 'balance' for your figure if you get the height right first. (See Standard Pattern Size Chart overleaf.)

CHOOSING YOUR FABRIC

For most people matching fabric and pattern is often a difficult decision.

I always start with the fabric first, knowing that if I like the colour and the 'feel' of the material, I can make up a very simple style and know that I will like the finished garment.

Once you have seen the fabric that you like you should, ideally, choose your pattern, take it home and correct the fitting – particularly the length – before you actually spend money on the material, as this can save a lot of waste and go a long way towards buying the other items that you will need to sew the garment.

STANDARD PATTERN SIZE CHART

IMPERIAL

TODDLERS

Toddler patterns are designed for a figure between that of a baby and a child. Toddlers' pants have a diaper allowance, dresses are shorter than the similar Child's size.

Size	½	1	2	3	4	
Breast or Chest	19	20	21	22	23	"
Waist	19	19½	20	20½	21	"
Finished Dress Length	14	15	16	17	18	"
Approx. Height	28	31	34	37	40	"

CHILDREN

Size	2	3	4	5	6	
Breast or Chest	21	22	23	24	25	"
Waist	20	20½	21	21½	22	"
Hip	—	—	24	25	26	"
Back Waist Length	8½	9	9½	10	10½	"
Finished Dress Length	18	19	20	22	24	"
Approx. Height	35	38	41	44	47	"

GIRLS

Girls' patterns are designed for the girl who has not yet begun to mature. See below for approximate heights without shoes.

Size	7	8	10	12	14	
Breast	26	27	28½	30	32	"
Waist	23	23½	24½	25½	26½	"
Hip	27	28	30	32	34	"
Back Waist Length	11½	12	12¾	13½	14¼	"
Approx. Height	50	52	56	58½	61	"

MISSES

Misses' patterns are designed for a well proportioned, and developed figure, about 5′5″ to 5′6″ without shoes.

Size	6	8	10	12	14	16	18	20	
Bust	30½	31½	32½	34	36	38	40	42	"
Waist	23	24	25	26½	28	30	32	34	"
Hip	32½	33½	34½	36	38	40	42	44	"
Back Waist Length	15½	15¾	16	16¼	16½	16¾	17	17¼	"

METRIC

TODDLERS

Toddler patterns are designed for a figure between that of a baby and a child. Toddlers' pants have a diaper allowance, dresses are shorter than the similar Child's size.

Size	½	1	2	3	4	
Breast or Chest	48	51	53	56	58	cm
Waist	48	50	51	52	53	cm
Finished Dress Length	35.5	38	40.5	43	46	cm
Approx. Height	71	79	87	94	102	cm

CHILDREN

Size	2	3	4	5	6	
Breast or Chest	53	56	58	61	64	cm
Waist	51	52	53	55	56	cm
Hip	—	—	61	64	66	cm
Back Waist Length	22	23	24	25.5	27	cm
Finished Dress Length	46	48	51	56	61	cm
Approx. Height	89	97	104	112	119	cm

GIRLS

Girls' patterns are designed for the girl who has not yet begun to mature. See below for approximate heights without shoes.

Size	7	8	10	12	14	
Breast	66	69	73	76	81	cm
Waist	58	60	62	65	67	cm
Hip	69	71	76	81	87	cm
Back Waist Length	29.5	31	32.5	34.5	36	cm
Approx. Height	127	132	142	149	155	cm

MISSES

Misses' patterns are designed for a well proportioned, and developed figure, about 1.65 m to 1.68 m without shoes.

Size	6	8	10	12	14	16	18	20	
Bust	78	80	83	87	92	97	102	107	cm
Waist	58	61	64	67	71	76	81	87	cm
Hip	83	85	88	92	97	102	107	112	cm
Back Waist Length	39.5	40	40.5	41.5	42	42.5	43	44	cm

IMPERIAL

SHORTER FITTING (HALF-SIZE)

Half-size patterns are for a fully developed figure with a short back waist length, about 5′2″ to 5′3″ without shoes.

Size	10½	12½	14½	16½	18½	20½	22½	24½	
Bust	33	35	37	39	41	43	45	47	″
Waist	27	29	31	33	35	37½	40	42½	″
Hip	35	37	39	41	43	45½	48	50½	″
Back Waist Length	15	15¼	15½	15¾	15⅞	16	16⅛	16¼	″

WOMEN

Women's patterns are designed for the larger, more fully mature figure, about 5′5″ to 5′6″ without shoes.

Size	38	40	42	44	46	48	50	
Bust	42	44	46	48	50	52	54	″
Waist	35	37	39	41½	44	46½	49	″
Hip	44	46	48	50	52	54	56	″
Back Waist Length	17¼	17⅜	17½	17⅝	17¾	17⅞	18	″

METRIC

SHORTER FITTING (HALF-SIZE)

Half-size patterns are for a fully developed figure with a short back waist length, about 1.57 m to 1.60 m without shoes.

Size	10.5	12.5	14.5	16.5	18.5	20.5	22.5	24.5	
Bust	84	89	94	99	104	109	114	119	cm
Waist	69	74	79	84	89	96	102	108	cm
Hip	89	94	99	104	109	116	122	128	cm
Back Waist Length	38	39	39.5	40	40.5	40.5	41	41.6	cm

WOMEN

Women's patterns are designed for the larger, more fully mature figure, about 1.65 m to 1.68 m without shoes.

Size	38	40	42	44	46	48	50	
Bust	107	112	117	122	127	132	137	cm
Waist	89	94	99	105	112	118	124	cm
Hip	112	117	122	127	132	137	142	cm
Back Waist Length	44	44	44.5	45	45	45.5	46	cm

FABRIC TIPS AND SNIPS

Garments that have gathers or drapes should be made in soft handling fabrics. Try them in the shop before you buy.

Suits, skirts and items that need a tailored look should be made in firm fabrics that press well.

Remember that Crease Resistant means that pressing will be more difficult.

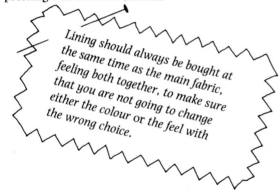

Lining should always be bought at the same time as the main fabric, feeling both together, to make sure that you are not going to change either the colour or the feel with the wrong choice.

Interfacing plays an important part in today's dressmaking. It is used to strengthen areas – such as buttonhole and button positions – and to help retain the shape and 'sharpen' the crisp edges of garments. It is used in conjunction with facings and collars, and comes in many different weights, suitable for different types of fabric. Ask to see them in the shop, whilst you have your fabric with you, and ask for help to choose the correct interfacing for your garment.

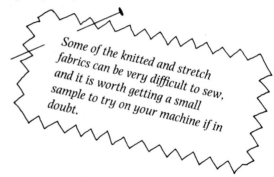

Some of the knitted and stretch fabrics can be very difficult to sew, and it is worth getting a small sample to try on your machine if in doubt.

Print and check fabrics should have 'mirrored' designs, so that, when you fold the fabric, the design and colours should lie over each other, again try this out in the shop.

If you do not like having to match checks, try cutting some parts of the garment 'on the cross', which makes for easier sewing, and can give a very creative effect.

Try to learn all the different fabric widths available, so that you can learn to buy economically for the garments you are making.

FABRIC PLANNING

Both woven and knitted fabrics can be bought in several different widths, some of which can be more economical to use than others.

If you have enjoyed manipulating the miniature patterns to explore pattern design you can also buy a special Fabric Requirement Planner that goes with the miniature patterns and allows you to plan how much fabric to buy, which width to look for, and how best to arrange the pattern pieces on to the selected fabric widths.

The planner reads off how much fabric you would need to make the garment full size. Details from Betty Foster, P.O. Box 28, Crewe.

The fabric widths most widely available are: 35–36 ins (90 cms); 44–45 ins (115 cms); 52–54 ins (135–140 cms); 58–60 ins (150 cms).

The following chart must only be used as a comparative guide to help you to buy fabric in different widths than those stated on pattern envelopes.

It is *strictly* only an estimate, and does not take into account matching of checks and other designs. It is a handy chart to have in your handbag when buying fabric in sales.

With the modern fabrics and finishes you must be careful to look closely at the possibility of the fabric 'shading' if you cut it in opposite directions along its length.

35"–36" (90 cm)	44"–45" (115 cm)	52"–54" (140 cm)	58"–60" (150 cm)
1¾ (1.60 m)	1⅜ (1.30 m)	1⅛ (1.05 m)	1 (0.95 m)
2 (1.85 m)	1⅝ (1.50 m)	1⅜ (1.30 m)	1¼ (1.15 m)
2¼ (2.10 m)	1¾ (1.60 m)	1½ (1.40 m)	1⅜ (1.30 m)
2½ (2.30 m)	2⅛ (1.95 m)	1¾ (1.60 m)	1⅝ (1.50 m)
2⅞ (2.65 m)	2¼ (2.10 m)	1⅞ (1.75 m)	1¾ (1.60 m)
3⅛ (2.90 m)	2½ (2.30 m)	2 (1.85 m)	1⅞ (1.75 m)
3⅜ (3.10 m)	2¾ (2.55 m)	2¼ (2.10 m)	2 (1.85 m)
3¾ (3.45 m)	2⅞ (2.65 m)	2⅜ (2.20 m)	2¼ (2.10 m)
4¼ (3.90 m)	3⅛ (2.90 m)	2⅝ (2.40 m)	2⅜ (2.20 m)
4½ (4.15 m)	3⅜ (3.10 m)	2¾ (2.55 m)	2⅝ (2.40 m)
4¾ (4.35 m)	3⅝ (3.35 m)	2⅞ (2.65 m)	2¾ (2.55 m)
5 (4.60 m)	3⅞ (3.55 m)	3⅛ (2.90 m)	2⅞ (2.65 m)

Fabric Widths Chart

Velvet and pile fabrics are easy to identify, and must always be cut in one direction, but we are also finding that many more fabrics need to be treated in this way.

To check fabric you should hold it as in Diagram 7.

Be particularly careful when calculating how much you need to buy with fabrics that have a 'nap'; these include velvet and other fabrics that 'stroke' in one direction. They must always be cut out with the pattern pieces going in the same direction. Nap fabrics are normally easy to identify because of their feel, but many modern fabrics, because of their finish, need to be treated in the same way. To check this, turn the fabric in such a way that you can see each direction side by side.

One-way designs must also be cut out so that all the pattern pieces face the same direction. Use the same method as described above to check this.

DIAGRAM 7

The wrong way to lay out pattern pieces on fabrics with nap or one-way designs

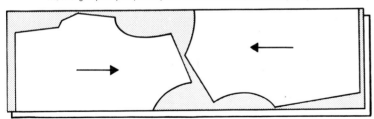

To check fabrics for nap or one-way designs

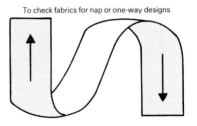

The right way to lay out pattern pieces on fabrics with nap or one-way designs

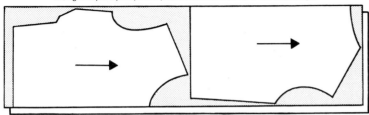

SEWING EQUIPMENT

THE MACHINE

Making clothes has been going on for a very long time ... certainly before the invention of the sewing machine ... and you do not need to have a new machine to be able to make a start.

Certainly you should not part with your old hand-machine, in part exchange, when you could pass it on to a youngster, or to someone who is just starting sewing, and needs to explore the subject without too big an outlay on equipment. Because of today's modern fabrics, with their stretch and unusual finishes, you could find that a new machine would bring great benefits to your dressmaking.

Look for a good machine dealer, who will be glad to give you ongoing advice at any time. When you go to look at machines take with you some scraps of fabric that you could possibly use in the future, and ask them to demonstrate on those. Try lifting the machine (although I strongly recommend a machine cabinet, if you have the room and can afford the price).

Look for a good forward and reverse stitch with easy controls. The zigzag stitch (which neatens the fabric edges) also produces the buttonhole stitch, and it should be easy to change to this whenever required.

Buttonholing is a very useful facility, but it takes practice, and you should try this out, on different fabrics, before buying your machine. I much prefer the 4- or 5-step buttonhole which does not require you to turn the work round when you are machining. These are the minimum requirements that you want in a new machine.

Other functions are available, special stitches for stretch fabrics, overlock and trimming, embroidery stitches, and these will be reflected in the price you pay. Your sewing machine will be the most expensive piece of equipment, so buy it carefully, treat it kindly, practise regularly, and maintain it carefully. Always keep the instruction book close at hand.

If the machine will not sew check first that you have threaded it up properly (both the top thread and the spool). Check the threading of the needle, and also that the needle is not bent or blunt.

Always buy good quality needles, and be prepared for a new needle for every garment, particularly with man-made fabrics. Find out about ball point needles (designed for knitted fabrics) and perfect stitch needles (which help to stop stitches from 'skipping').

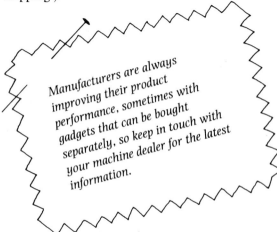

Manufacturers are always improving their product performance, sometimes with gadgets that can be bought separately, so keep in touch with your machine dealer for the latest information.

TAPE MEASURE

A good tape measure will be vital to your pattern work, and general dressmaking. I recommend the Analogical tape, which does not have long brass ends (you will need to bend the tape to measure round corners), and it is marked with both inches and centimetres on both sides, which makes conversion from one to the other very much easier.

SCISSORS

Always buy the best quality that you can afford. Ideally you should have two pairs, one for cutting out and a smaller pair (with sharp points) for trimming and cutting buttonholes. Cutting-out scissors should be tried out in the shop, making sure that the weight and feel of them is comfortable in your hands.

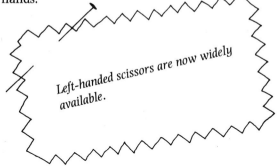

Left-handed scissors are now widely available.

SEWING THREAD

Always buy branded sewing threads, which have been specially tested and prepared for the domestic sewing machines. Match the thread to your fabric, not only in colour but also in content, so that it will wash exactly as the fabric you are sewing. You can buy 100% cotton thread, cotton and polyester thread, 100% polyester thread, and, more rarely, pure silk thread.

You can also buy special threads for 'top-stitching', and for doing machine embroidery. Metallic and 'glitter' threads are also now becoming available and you should watch for these in the shops. Beware of the large 'cops' of thread often found on the markets, which have come from manufacturing machines and are very different from the domestic threads that you need at home.

PINS

Stainless steel pins are essential, being both fine and sharp, but they must not be left in the fabric for any longer than is necessary, and you should *never* press over them.

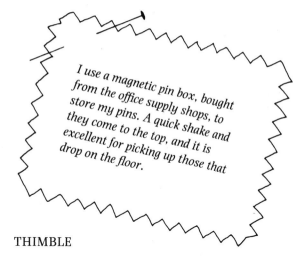

I use a magnetic pin box, bought from the office supply shops, to store my pins. A quick shake and they come to the top, and it is excellent for picking up those that drop on the floor.

THIMBLE

I do very little hand sewing. Hems, hooks and eyes, belt loops, buttons and general repairs, but I find a thimble to be most useful, and it certainly saves a lot of wear-and-tear on your fingers.

HAND SEWING NEEDLES

Buy a packet of assorted shapes and sizes, which usually come with a needle threader, so that you are ready for anything.

HOOKS AND EYES, PRESS STUDS, ELASTIC

Keep an assortment readily to hand, so that you are not always buying new cards for every job.

BUTTONS ETC

Keep buttons, and other small objects, in a screw-top jar, so that you can see at a glance what you are looking for.

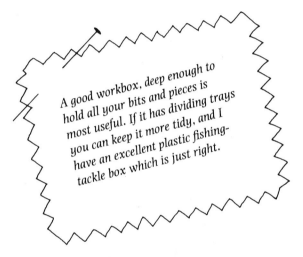

A good workbox, deep enough to hold all your bits and pieces is most useful. If it has dividing trays you can keep it more tidy, and I have an excellent plastic fishing-tackle box which is just right.

IRON AND IRONING BOARD

Your iron, whether it be traditional or 'steam', must have a good thermostat control. The temperature at which you press is vital for many fabrics, and you should *always* do a test press, on left-over fabric, before attempting to touch your garment. If your ironing board has a sleeve board attachment you will find it useful, and it is worth buying as a separate item if you do a lot of sewing.

When pressing you should try to have a stool or chair *under* the board to support the weight of your garment, so that things like hems are not stretched by the weight of the garment hanging down.

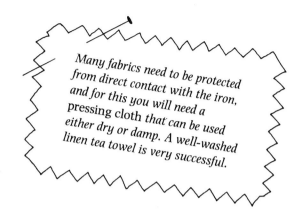

Many fabrics need to be protected from direct contact with the iron, and for this you will need a pressing cloth that can be used either dry or damp. A well-washed linen tea towel is very successful.

HOW MUCH FABRIC SHOULD YOU BUY?

The ready-printed commercial patterns tell you on the back how much fabric to buy in the stated widths. This amount is, of course, assuming that you are the correct size for the pattern without any adjustments, and you can sometimes save on your fabric purchase if you know that the patterns need shortening.

If you are making your own patterns, or even going to use different widths than those given on the pattern envelopes, you would find it useful to make yourself some cheap 'fabric planners'. My set is still good after many years of use, and has proved to be a valuable investment.

I bought 6 metres (or 6 yards) of very cheap knitted fabric and cut it into lengths as follows:
Piece 1 45 cm (18 ins) wide × 3 metres (or 3 yards) long.
Piece 2 57 cm (22½ ins) wide × 3 metres (or 3 yards) long.
Piece 3 67 cm (27 ins) wide × 3 metres (or 3 yards) long.
Piece 4 75 cms (30 ins) wide × 3 metres (or 3 yards) long.
Each length represents 3 metres (or 3 yards) of the *folded* fabric in the fabric widths 90 cms (36 ins), 115 cms (45 ins), 135 cms (54 ins), and 150 cms (60 ins).

When I see fabric that I like I check the width, then get out the appropriate 'fabric planner' and pin my pattern pieces on to it, before measuring off how much to buy.

It has made changing from one width to another very easy, and has saved me a lot of money over the years because I never buy more than I need.

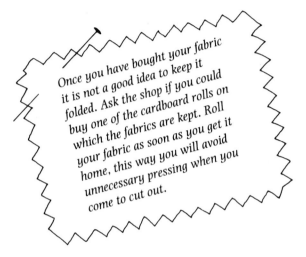

Once you have bought your fabric it is not a good idea to keep it folded. Ask the shop if you could buy one of the cardboard rolls on which the fabrics are kept. Roll your fabric as soon as you get it home, this way you will avoid unnecessary pressing when you come to cut out.

CUTTING OUT

Making a Board

It is very much easier to cut out if you have a good flat surface. A lot of people use the floor, because they haven't got a big table, or, if they have, it is the best dining-table and they are nervous about marking it with pins and scissors.

I have made my own cutting-out board: Buy a piece of hardboard from a D.I.Y. shop, where they will cut it for you to 152 cms × 122 cms (5ft × 4 ft), which is a convenient size. One side of the hardboard is rough, and, to this side, I have stuck a piece of *felt*. I can now place this side down on my table, and can turn my 'Cutting Board' round as I am working, without marking the table top. The shiny side of the hardboard makes an excellent cutting surface and I can draw information on to

it, e.g. buttonhole distances, hem depths, direct cross-way lines etc. I can also turn the board over, so that the felt side is on top and I can then pin pattern pieces to it when I am making and checking patterns. It stores away under a single bed or behind a wardrobe when not in use.

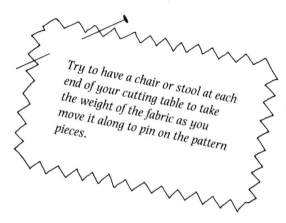

Try to have a chair or stool at each end of your cutting table to take the weight of the fabric as you move it along to pin on the pattern pieces.

Pin the pattern firmly to the fabric – preferably at right angles to the edges being cut – and keep the pins well clear of the scissors. Leave the pattern pinned to the fabric until you are ready to handle each piece. Always be sure to transfer pattern markings that will help you when it comes to the sewing.

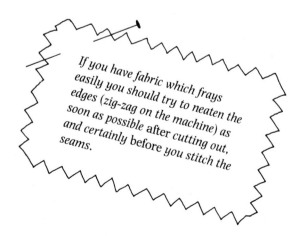

If you have fabric which frays easily you should try to neaten the edges (zig-zag on the machine) as soon as possible after cutting out, and certainly before you stitch the seams.

SEWING TECHNIQUES

1 SEAMS

The first thing you must learn to do in dressmaking is how to stitch two pieces of fabric together so that they will look good, wear well, and make the garment fit. The three seams that you are most likely to use are:

The Flat Seam, which is pressed open.

The French Seam, used for fine and delicate fabrics, and also when you want a neat inside finish, with added strength.

The Lap and Fell Seam, used for reversible and quilted fabrics.

The patterns will always tell you the amount of seam allowance that has been allowed, and you should follow this instruction carefully.

The Flat Seam

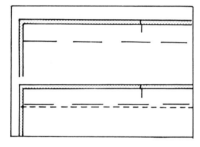
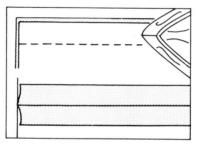

1. The two pieces of fabric are usually placed with the right sides together and the edges level. The seam allowance should be tacked and then machined just inside the tacking line.

2. The tacking is removed and the seam is then first pressed flat, with both edges together.
The seam is then pressed open.

The French Seam

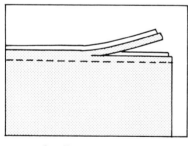
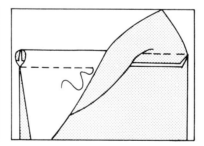

3. Stitch half the seam allowance with the wrong side of the fabrics together then trim away at least half the seam.

4. Fold the stitched fabric so that the right sides are together then stitch the second part of the seam, which completely encloses the first seam edges.

Lap and Fell Seam

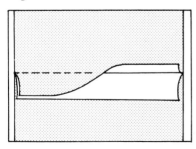
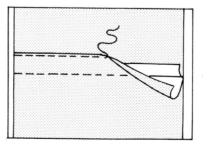

5. With the wrong sides together stitch the first seam, then trim one side only back to the stitching line.

6. Turn the remaining seam edge over the stitching line, turn the edge under, and stitch into place.

Key to the Diagrams

Right Side of the Fabric   Wrong Side of the Fabric   Interfacing

2 SEAM FINISHES

Woven fabrics will fray – some more than others – and this must be prevented if the garment is going to wash and wear well. If the inside of the garment will be seen at any time, as in an unlined jacket or blouse, the seams must also look neat and tidy and, consequently you should neaten the seam edges by one of the many methods available.

Knitted fabrics do not fray, and therefore can be made up without seam neatening, and many of the ready-made garments in this type of fabric do not have the usual open-seam. Usually both edges are placed together, stitched, and then the two edges are oversewn together. You should look at the inside making of garments in the shops and see if your machine has the facility to copy this method.

If you use this method for knitted fabrics you will only need a small seam allowance, otherwise it will be too bulky on the inside of the garment.

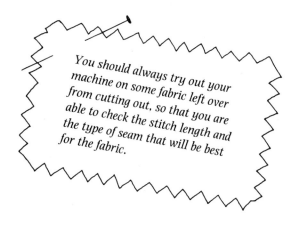

You should always try out your machine on some fabric left over from cutting out, so that you are able to check the stitch length and the type of seam that will be best for the fabric.

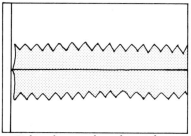

1. Pinking shears can be used to cut the edges of the seams, which helps prevent fraying.

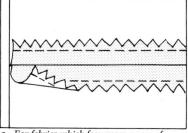

2. For fabrics which fray more a row of machine stitching can be done inside the pinked edge.

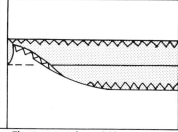

3. The zig-zag stitch, available on many sewing machines, has made seam neatening very easy. Try to do as many edges as possible as soon as you have cut out the garment.

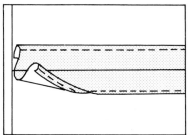

4. If the fabric is not too bulky you can turn each seam edge under and stitch either side. I find this easier to do before stitching the seam.

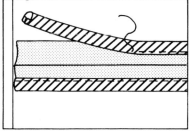

5. Bias binding can be bought and used to bind each edge of the seams. It can be a decorative contrast on unlined coats.

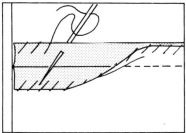

6. Hand oversewing takes time but is a very effective method of neatening seams.

3 FACINGS

Some parts of a garment will require *facings* to neaten the raw edges. Facings are merely a small section of the main pattern piece, which can be stitched to the right side of the garment, following the edge outline, and then turned inside the garment to give a very neat appearance.

Many of these facings go around curved edges, and it is very easy to stretch them if you are not careful.

You can stitch around the edge of the garment before you attach the facing (this is called stay-stitching and stops the stretch) and you can also use *interfacing* to help keep the shape and to add support and crispness to the garment.

Vilene make a very extensive range of interfac-ings for a vast range of fabrics and you should select your interfacing carefully. You can buy both Iron-on and Sew-In, and, whichever you choose to use, it should be attached to the *facing* and *not* to the garment.

Facings need not be in the same material as the main garment, and a good quality lining can often be preferred, particularly with thick fabrics.

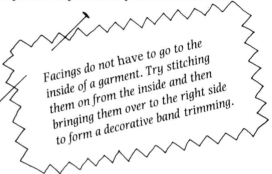

Facings do not have to go to the inside of a garment. Try stitching them on from the inside and then bringing them over to the right side to form a decorative band trimming.

Neck and Armhole Facings

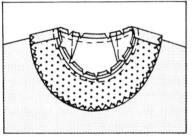

1. With the shoulder seams joined, the facing (with interfacing attached) is stitched to the neckline. The neck seam should be trimmed and layered to reduce the bulk, and also clipped to allow the facing to roll to the inside.

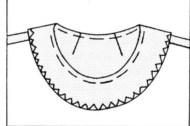

2. The facing is taken to the inside of the garment and the outer edge is neatened.

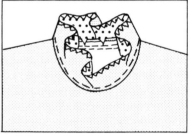

3. To improve the facing a row of machining can be done from the inside edge, catching the seam allowance to the facing. I find a zipper foot very useful for this operation.

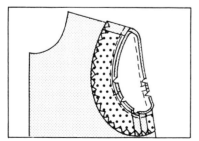

4. Sleeve edge facings on sleeveless dresses are attached in the same way as for necklines.

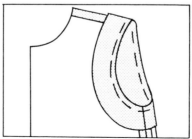

5. The sleeve facing is turned to the inside of the garment.

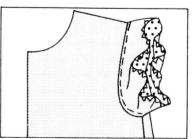

6. As in step 3 for the neckline facing an additional row of machining prevents the facing rolling to the outside.

Jacket or Blouse Facings

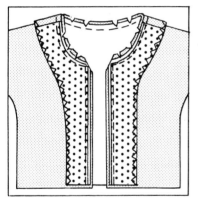

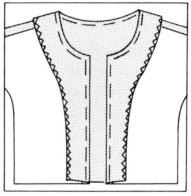

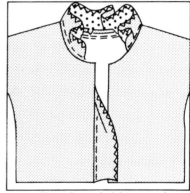

1. Interfacing is attached to the facing, which is then stitched to the front and neck edges of the garment.

2. The facing is turned to the inside and the outer edges neatened.

3. An additional row of machining can be done to secure the facing to the inside seam allowance, which should have been layered to prevent bulk.

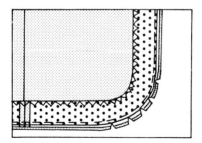

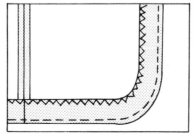

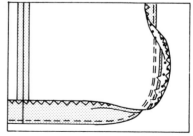

4. The bottom of a garment can sometimes have a facing instead of a hem, and this is attached continuously with the fronts and neckline. Curved edges must be clipped before turning to the right side.

5. The outer edge is neatened, and will finally be hand caught to the main garment.

6. The extra machine stitching of the facing to seam from the inside edge will ensure a good finished edge.

4 DARTS

Flat fabric has to take on the shape of the body, and this is usually done by a combination of shaped cutting and *darts*. Darts are needed to allow a flat piece of fabric to fit the bust, go in at the waist and come out again at the hips. They are needed to allow the shoulders to fit and then to let the fabric come out again over the shoulder blades. They are particularly needed in women's garments to allow the flat fabric to fit the bust. They can occur in the middle of a piece or they can start on an outer edge, and they can be curved or straight.

If you work with the pattern section at the be-ginning of the book you will know that darts play a major part in garment design, and they cannot be ignored.

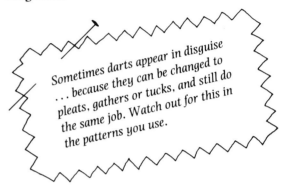

Sometimes darts appear in disguise ... because they can be changed to pleats, gathers or tucks, and still do the same job. Watch out for this in the patterns you use.

Darts – Front

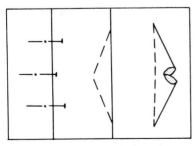

1. *Bust shaping darts must always be absolutely even from each side. They must also always be in the correct position for the wearer.*

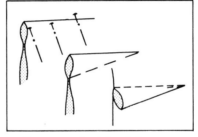

2. *Always pin and tack darts before machining them, starting from the outer edge and finishing at the point.*

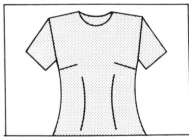

3. *Waist darts occur in both the fronts and backs of many garments.*

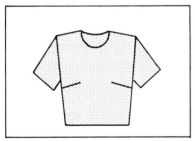

4. *Pin, tack, and machine the darts, then clip the centre before pressing.*

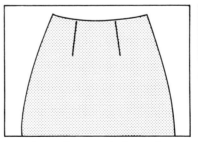

5. *In skirts and trousers the darts go from the waist downwards.*

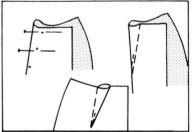

6. *Pin, tack and machine the darts in the direction indicated in the patterns.*

Darts – Back

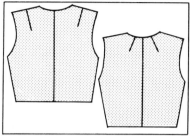 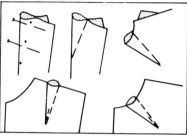 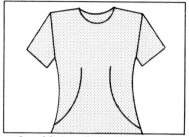

1. At the back of a garment you can have either shoulder darts or neck darts, and, in some cases, you will find both. The addition of a small neck dart can considerably improve the fit of collars for many people.

2. Pinning, tacking and machining.

3. Curved darts can be found in many fashions.

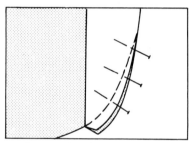 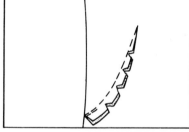 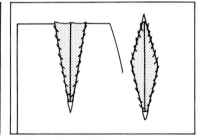

4. Always machine from the outer edge to the point.

5. Clip the seam created by this dart to allow it to lie better when pressed.

6. If your fabric is thick you can trim and neaten the edges of the dart before pressing them open.

5 ZIP FASTENERS

Whatever did we do before the invention of the zip? It certainly revolutionised the making of clothes, but it still is something that many people use not very successfully.

The trouble is that you need to *practise*. Buy a small zip (15 cms/6 ins), get a small piece of fabric, seam it to leave just enough left for the zip and then put the zip in and take it out *every time* you use your machine. You will soon become very expert. Good quality zips are essential, strong enough for the job they are to do, and, because they often come in 5 cm (2 in) jumps you should err on the long side rather than the short side. Most skirt and jean zips break only because they are too short to allow the garment to open to go over the hips. I always replace them with a zip 2.5 cms (1 in) longer.

Most zips are not seen in the garment – indeed there are some excellent 'invisible' zips available which require quite experienced sewing to put them into the garment. Some zips form part of the decoration, particularly in bright contrast colours.

I know many people who always put in their zips by hand, but I have never done this, perhaps because I always recommend that the zip should go in right at the beginning – whilst the garment is flat and not stitched up – which is the way most manufacturers do this particular operation.

Method 1. Edge to Edge Method

Use a zipper foot on your machine

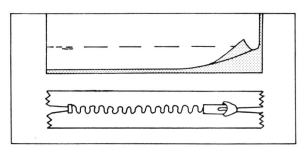

1. Stitch the seam to the base of the zip, having measured the opening required plus *the top seam allowance. Tack the zip opening and press the seam open.*

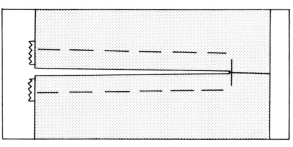

3. Tack the zip into position and remove the pins.

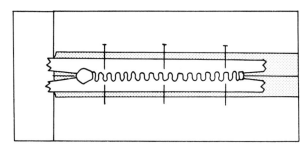

2. Pin the zip carefully, and evenly over the opening.

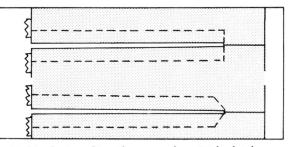

4. Machine the zip, making either a squared or pointed end at the base of the zip when machining.

Method 2. The Overlap Method

A zipper foot is essential for this method, when you will need to stitch close to the teeth of the zip.

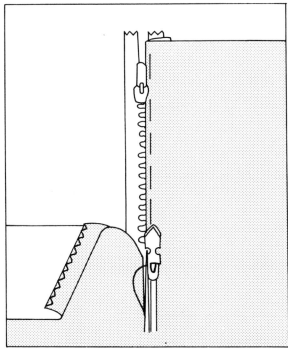

1. Starting from the base of the zip, machine the first side, with the other side of the fabric well folded out of the way.

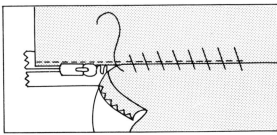

2. Bring the other side into position and tack or pin into place.

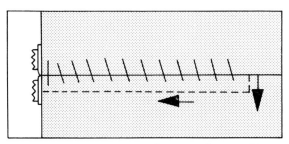

3. Starting from the bottom point, where stage 1 began, machine 4 or 5 stitches across the bottom, then turn and stitch up the remaining side.

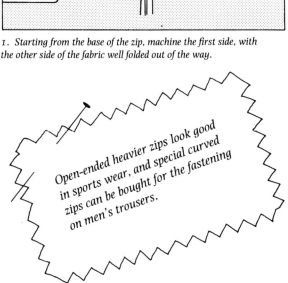

Open-ended heavier zips look good in sports wear, and special curved zips can be bought for the fastening on men's trousers.

6 BINDING

I have always thought that binding is perhaps the most useful of all the sewing techniques.

First it can be used to neaten raw edges and to stop them from fraying, obviously, whilst you are doing this, you can take advantage of using contrast fabric or even using a different type of fabric for the binding material.

Binding can be used around necklines, instead of facings, and it can continue around the neck to form a tie at either the front or back neck opening.

I have always found it best to use binding for sleeveless dresses, rather than attaching a facing to the armhole. I get a closer fit, the armhole is much more comfortable to wear, and the facings never poke out in wearing.

You can also cut your own bias binding from contrast or matching fabric, but you must take care to do this on the absolute crossway grain of the fabric, otherwise it will twist.

Finally, because the method used for sewing on the binding is similar to putting on waistbands and cuffs, I find that I get lots of practice in the method.

Single Binding

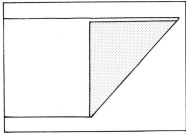

1. To cut bias strips for use as binding you must first fold your fabric at right angles to the warp (up and down) direction.
Pin, tack, or chalk mark this folded line.

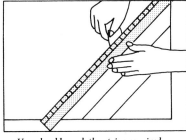

2. You should mark the strips required before cutting them carefully.

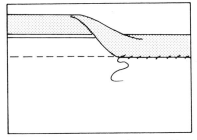

3. To join strips of bias fabric place the ends as indicated, stitch the seam, and then trim the corners which are left when you open it out and press.

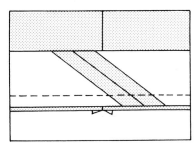

4. Stitch the binding to the right side of the garment, as you would a normal seam.

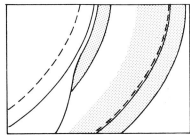

5. Bring the binding over to the wrong side of the garment, fold in the remaining edge, and hand stitch to the original machine line.

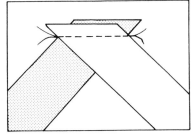

6. Alternatively you can fold the binding over to be below the original stitching line, then, using a zipper foot on the machine, 'stitch-in-the-ditch' of the original machine line from the right side of the garment.

Double Binding

Double, or folded, binding can be used either for additional strength or decorative emphasis.

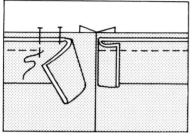

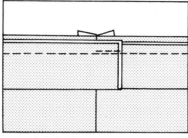

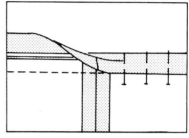

1. The folded binding is stitched to the garment, with the join located preferably by a seam. Note the fold back on one edge, which avoids a bulky seam in the binding.

2. Stitch the binding to the edge on the right side of the fabric.

3. Fold the binding over to the wrong side, and use pins to avoid twisting the binding as you fold it over.

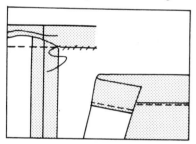

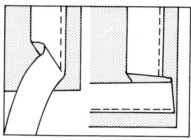

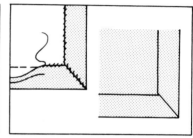

4. Hand catch the remaining edge to the original stitching line or 'stitch-in-the-ditch' as for single binding.

5. Round corners are easier to bind. If, however, you have a squared corner, stitch down one edge, and then fold the 'mitred' corner of the binding before continuing with the bottom edge.

6. You can machine across the 'mitred' corner and trim away the fabric, or you can fold the 'mitre' inside the binding, before hand catching the binding to the original stitching line.

You can buy excellent bias binding in the shops, in a wide range of colours and several widths.

7 BOUND SLEEVES AND TIE NECKLINES

The use of ties, whether knotted or bows, gives a very effective fashion detail, and avoids the use of buttons and buttonholes, hooks and eyes, and zips.

The fabric used for these ties must always be cut on the crossway grain (the bias) of the fabric, and the binding can be as narrow or as wide as you require.

It is always important to make your strips long enough to do the job, and you should measure the neckline and add enough for the bow-ends, similarly for the bottom of sleeves.

The ends which tie are going to be stitched and turned through to the right side of the fabric, and you can finish the ends either as 'square' or 'pointed', and, with very narrow binding, you can simply knot the ends.

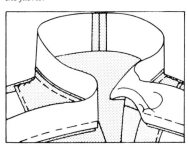

1. *Sleeves. Gather the sleeve bottom to the required size, then stitch one edge of the binding to the right side, from edge to edge. Stitch together each edge of the tie ends remaining and turn them to the right side of the fabric.*

2. *As with single binding, turn the remaining raw edge of the binding under and hand catch to the original machine stitching line.*

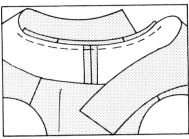

3. *Necklines. Starting from the centre back neck stitch one edge of the tie neck binding to the neckline.*

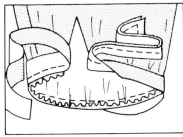

4. *Stitch together the edges of the remaining tie ends, and turn the ties through to the right side of the fabric.*

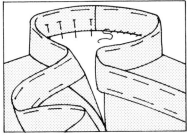

5. *Use tacking and pins to fold over and position the neck binding, then hand catch the remaining edge to the original stitching line.*

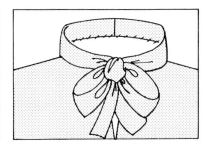

6. *The ends can be tied into a bow, or knotted, as required.*

You should try to get any joins in the binding strips to coincide either with the centre back neck or the shoulder seams of a neckline, and with the underarm seam of a sleeve.

8 SLASH OPENING

If you are having problems with zips, and particularly if you are making garments in stretch fabrics, which you can get on and off without a long zip opening, but for which you require a neck opening to avoid stretching the neckline, you can use the same method as is used for the placket opening on some cuffed sleeves.

The method is illustrated for a front opening, where there is no centre front seam.

With either a centre front or back seam no facings would be necessary, as the seam would simply turn to the inside of the garment and you would proceed as for binding sleeves or neck ties.

Stitch it to the *inside* of the garment first, then bring it to the outside of the garment at Step 3, and top stitch the facing into place on the right side of the garment.

Beading, quilting, or embroidery could make this facing something special.

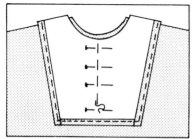

1. You will require a facing deep enough to go below the opening, and with the edges neatened. Interfacing is recommended down the centre front, which should be carefully tacked to ensure exact positioning.

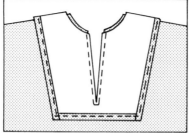

2. Stitch down either side of the tacked line, either to a 'V' at the bottom or turning using no more than three small machine stitches before coming up the other side. Cut down the tacking line very carefully.

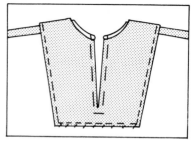

3. Turn the facing to the inside of the garment.

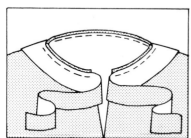

4. Button and loops can finish the neckline edge, or a hook and eye fastening, otherwise a binding can be used stitched first to the neckline.

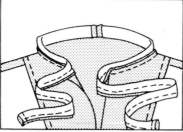

5. The tie ends are then stitched and turned to the right side.

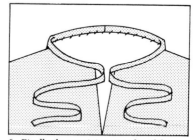

6. Finally the remaining raw edge of the binding is turned in and stitched to the first machine line of the neckline.

If you are using facings you can achieve a very decorative effect by using a contrast or more elaborate fabric for the facing.

9 COLLARS

A plain neckline can be completely transformed by the addition of a collar, and on page 13 you will see how easy it is to make a collar pattern for any neckline.

Some collars have a folded outside edge, whilst others are cut in two pieces with a seamed edge around the outside. You can always change from one to the other if you find it more economic in the use of fabric, particularly as the under-collar could be cut from a different fabric if you are short of material.

A suitable interfacing improves the look of most collars and you should choose this carefully when you buy your fabric.

If the collar is cut with a top and bottom section it will always lie very much better if the under-collar is cut on the *crossway* of the material.

It will also lie very much better if the under-collar is cut fractionally smaller than the top collar around the *outer* edges only, as this stops the rolling that can occur with some fabrics. Decorative top stitching can add detail to a collar, and can be repeated on the cuffs and pockets of suitable garments.

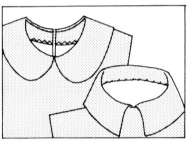

1. Collars can be made in two halves, as used with centre back openings or they can be on one piece, as used on front fastening garments.

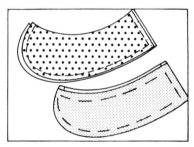

2. Collars in two halves are seamed around the outer edge, leaving the neckline open, and with interfacing stitched in with the seams. The seams should be trimmed and layered after stitching to reduce the bulk.

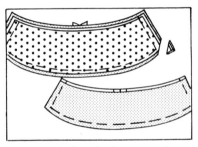

3. One-piece collars often have a seam in the centre back of the under collar, although this is not necessary. The two collar pieces (with interfacing) are stitched, right sides together, around the outer edge. Trim and layer the seams before turning the collar to the right side.

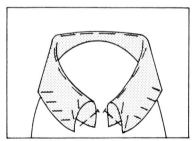

4. An all-in-one shirt-style collar should be pressed and shaped to give it the correct 'roll' line using either a special pressing ham, or the end of a sleeve board.

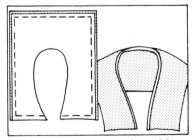

5. Sailor collars are very popular, and do not usually require interfacing, the outer edges are stitched, and the seams trimmed and layered, before turning the collar to the right side.

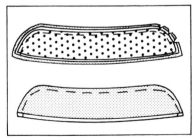

6. The mandarin (or grandad) collar is again made in two pieces, with interfacing between the layers. The outer (top) edge is stitched, clipped on any curves, and layered before turning the collar to the right side.

Collars can be in the same fabric as the garment, or they can be a complete contrast.

Many necklines, particularly on small children's garments, are best if the finished edge is completely bound.

It is interesting to note that the true shirt collar is a combination of the mandarin and straight collar, and you could perhaps try this out as an idea for yourself.

10 SHIRT COLLARS

The shirt collar can be made in two ways. Either with a separate collar band and top collar *or* as a shaped all-in-one collar.

Although many interfacings are available it is not often possible to achieve, at home, the very crisp fused collars that you buy in ready-made shirts, because special fusing equipment is required.

You should experiment with this type of collar, using different interfacings, until you find a finish that is acceptable.

In Diagram 4, Technique 9, you will see how the roll of a shirt collar is pressed, and you will perhaps find it useful to put a row of machining along this roll line to help retain the shape and correct fold.

This type of collar always goes right to the front edges of the shirt or blouse, and is not used when a collar and rever is required.

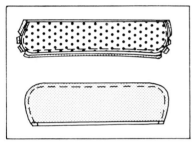

1. This shows the top collar portion of a two-piece collar, which is stitched around the outer edge, with the seam, clipped, layered and trimmed before turning to the right side.

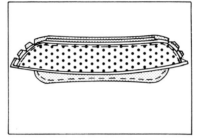

2. The bottom section of the collar (the mandarin collar) is now placed on either side of the top collar, making a 'sandwich' of the top collar. This is then stitched around the edge, as illustrated, then the seam line is clipped, layered and trimmed, before turning to the right side.

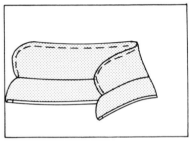

3. When the collar is fully turned the bottom edge remains open ready to be stitched to the neckline.

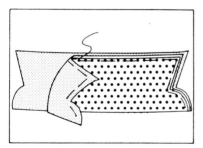

4. The all-in-one shirt-style collar is made exactly as the collars in Technique 9. Particular care must be taken when machining round the curved ends.

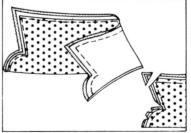

5. Once stitched the seams must be clipped and trimmed.

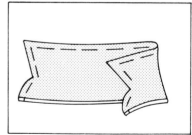

6. The collar is then turned to the right side ready to be attached to the neckline.

11 ATTACHING COLLARS

Collars should always be stitched to necklines before the facings are attached, this is to ensure accurate positioning. It is much easier to attach collars, and neckline facings, *before* the side seams of a garment are stitched, and you should try to do this whenever possible.

Always clearly identify the centre back and centre front of your garment and your collar. Pin either the centre front or centre back of each to- gether carefully and then proceed to pin and tack to either side to ensure accuracy at each edge.

The methods illustrated show the use of facings and the use of a facing fold-back combined with a back neck binding.

You can always make collars that are detach- able, which can be very useful if they require fre- quent washing. To do this make up the collar as normal and then bind the neck edge, using a bind- ing which will be wide enough to allow you to stitch it to the inside of the neck of the garment.

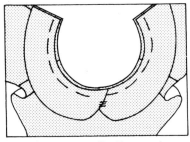

1. With a two-piece collar (for example a garment with a centre-back opening) tack the collar to the neckline, noting the small overlap which will keep the centre front edges together when the seam allowance has been stitched.

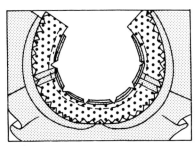

2. Stitch the facing to the neckline, trimming and clipping the seam to allow it to turn easily to the inside of the garment.

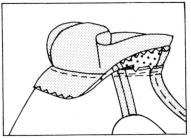

3. Tack the facing to the inside of the garment, and machine another row of stitching through the facing and the seam allowance.

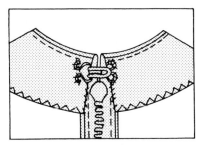

4. To finish the back neckline, fold the facing to the zip tape and hand catch in place. Stitch a hook and eye fastening to close the top of the zip.

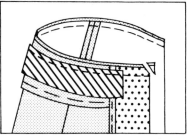

5. A front or back fastening garment often does not require a back-neck facing. The collar is stitched to the neckline to the centre front or centre back points, the front facing is then folded back over the collar, and a binding strip is stitched to the rest of the neckline, as illustrated, continuing over the facing.

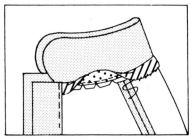

6. When the facing is turned to the right side the binding is then used to neaten the remaining neckline, using either a hand or machine stitch as preferred.

12 ADDITIONAL METHODS OF ATTACHING COLLARS

Diagrams 1–3 illustrate a method used when a collar and rever is required, and the front facing is cut to fold back to the shoulder seam line.

Diagrams 4–6 illustrate how collars, such as the mandarin/grandad, and shirt collar are put on to the front ends.

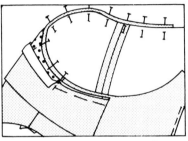

1. The under collar only is pinned and stitched to the back neckline, as far as the shoulder seam on each side, and both collar edges are stitched to the neckline from the shoulder seam to the centre front position.

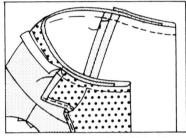

2. The front facings are then folded to the right side of the garment, with the shoulder seam of the facing folded over. This is then stitched to the neckline edge, and the seams should be clipped, layered and trimmed.

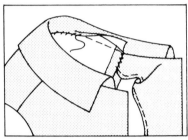

3. The facing is turned to the inside of the garment, and the remaining collar edge, across the back neckline, is hand stitched to the original machine stitching line. The facing shoulder seam is also hand stitched to the shoulder seam of the garment.

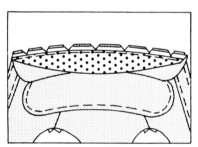

4. With a mandarin, grandad, or shirt collar, the under collar is first stitched to the neckline of the garment.

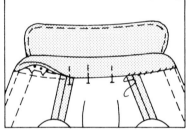

5. The remaining collar edge is then pinned and hand stitched to the original machine-stitching line.

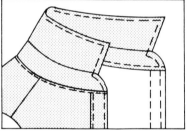

6. Using the method for the second stage of binding, when you stitch from the right side 'in-the-ditch' of the first machining, you can secure the inside collar edge by machine. Top stitching around the collar edge can also produce a good effect.

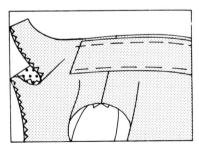

7. If the garment has a back facing, in addition to a front facing, you should first stitch both edges of the collar to the neckline of the garment.

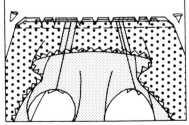

8. Stitch the shoulder seams of the back facing to the front facing, and then stitch the complete facing to the neckline, completely encasing the collar. Trim, clip, and layer the seam allowance.

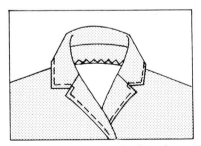

9. The collar and rever can be effectively top stitched, if required.

13 ROLL COLLARS

Roll collars can be cut to any depth that is in fashion. The most important factor in making a roll collar is that the fabric *must* be cut on the perfect crossway grain of the fabric, otherwise it will not roll successfully, and will twist when you try to sew it to the garment.

The length of the collar is the size of the neck edge, plus a seam allowance at either end.

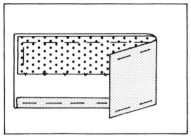

1. To prepare the collar, attach the interfacing and turn a small hem at one edge.

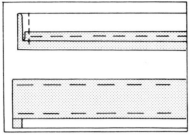

2. Fold the collar, as illustrated, and stitch the two ends.
Turn the collar to the right side, which leaves the seam allowance free to be stitched to the neckline.

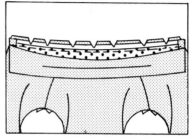

3. Stitch the collar to the neck edge and trim and clip the seam allowance.

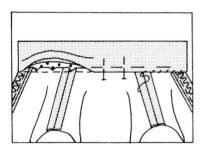

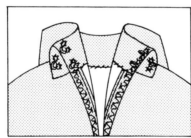

4. Pin and stitch the remaining edge to the original first machine line.

5. Stitch hooks and eyes to the rolled-over collar, as illustrated.

It is possible to buy a very light-weight stretch interfacing, which can be used very successfully if you want to use it in this type of collar.

14 CUFFS

Cuffs are often used in dressmaking, particularly on shirts and blouses, and there are several different ways of doing this particular technique.

Because cuffs fit the wrist it must be possible to open them and this is usually done with the aid of a button and buttonhole, although hooks and eyes, press studs, Velcro fastening, and the new snap fastenings (which look like buttons on the outside) can also be used.

Interfacing should always be used in cuffs, to help retain shape and crispness, and to support whatever type of fastening you select to use.

The bottom of the sleeve has to have an opening to allow you to get your hand through, and this opening is placed on the *back* line of the sleeve.

The two methods illustrated for making and attaching cuffs are widely used in ready-made manufacturing.

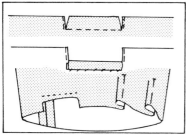

1. For this method a small hem of 2.5 cms (1 in) is stitched on the bottom of the sleeve, at the back sleeve position. The sleeve bottom must then be either pleated or gathered to a size that will allow you to get your hand through comfortably.

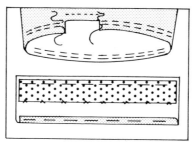

2. The gathered, or pleated edge now gives you the exact length of the cuff you require, which must be cut with a seam allowance at each end. The cuffs can be cut to any required width.
Interfacing should be used in the cuff, and a small hem stitched on one of the long edges.

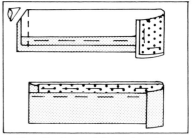

3. The cuff is then made by stitching the two end seams, clipping and trimming the seams, and turning the cuff to the right side, as illustrated.

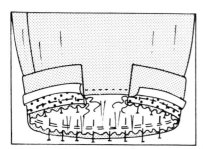

4. The interfaced edge of the cuff is then stitched to the bottom of the sleeve.

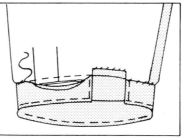

5. On the inside of the sleeve the remaining cuff edge is hand stitched to the original machine line.
Alternatively it can be machined 'in the ditch' from the right side.
A top stitched finish can be used.

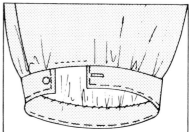

6. Button and buttonhole complete the cuff.

Alternative Method

Many patterns have a placket opening cut, which has to be either faced or bound. In this case the sleeve is either pleated or gathered to the actual finished wrist size. The cuff is cut to actual wrist size *plus* 5 cms (2 ins) at one end and a seam allowance at the other.

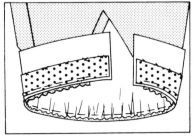

7. One half of the cuff is interfaced and this edge is stitched to the bottom of the sleeve.

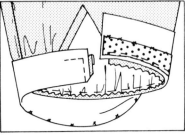

8. The hem on the remaining edge is folded over, and the wrap-under end is stitched, as illustrated, the remaining end is seamed.

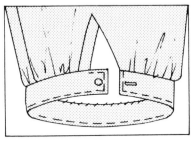

9. The cuff is turned to the right side, the remaining edge hand stitched into place, and button and buttonhole added.

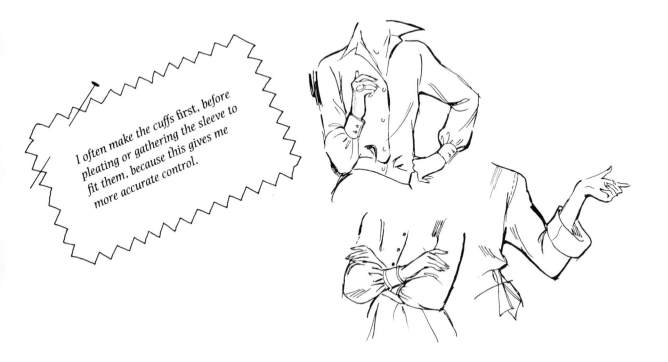

I often make the cuffs first, before pleating or gathering the sleeve to fit them, because this gives me more accurate control.

15 WAISTBANDS

I am always getting requests for help with waistbands, and the fitting of the skirts and trousers to which they are attached. Surprisingly it is the waistband that is causing a lot of the fitting problems.

Your *actual* waist position is a very finely defined position on your body, and if you tie a piece of string or tape much tighter than you would wear a belt it will settle exactly in your true waist position.

Now look carefully at your figure, and you will see that *immediately* above the string your circumference measurement is starting to increase ... *so*,

how can a band that fits your waist possibly fit even 2.5 cms (1 in) higher up?

The same thing happens below the waist, and therefore you must either be prepared to make the waistbands shaped *or* to make them fit your bigger measurement, *or*, best of all, to do what I always recommend, *stop using waistbands* and change to using *curved petersham*, which sits inside the skirt and makes it fit better and look superb.

If you have skirts which are 'ruckling' across the back waist try tucking the waistband *down* to the inside of the skirt and you will see immediately what I mean.

Method 1. Using Curved petersham. For either a centre front, centre back, *or* side zip.

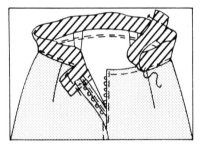
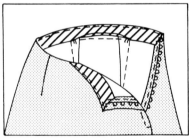

2. The petersham is then turned to the inside of the garment, which rolls the top seam over the edge, and completely neatens the seam edges. Hooks and eyes are then attached to each end of the petersham.
NOTE. *Belt-carrying tags can be stitched in at step one, and completed on to the right side of the fabric.*

1. Look carefully at your curved petersham to establish which is the inside (smaller) curve. With a small turn back at each end, the inside curve is stitched to the top, right side, of the skirt or trouser.

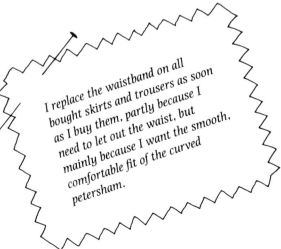

I replace the waistband on all bought skirts and trousers as soon as I buy them, partly because I need to let out the waist, but mainly because I want the smooth, comfortable fit of the curved petersham.

Method 2. Fabric Waistband

The waistband is cut to the waist size plus a seam allowance at one end, and an underwrap at the other, exactly as for the cuff method.

Half the waistband should be interfaced *or* preferably you should use the new *Fold-a-Band* interfacing, which comes in packets with complete interfacing instructions.

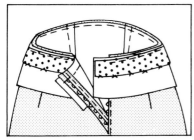

1. One edge of the waistband is stitched to the garment, with the seam allowance at one end and underwrap at the other.

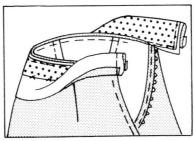

2. With a seam allowance turned under on the remaining edge the two short ends are stitched.

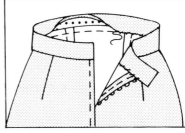

3. The waistband is turned to the right side, and the remaining edge is hand stitched to the original machining line.

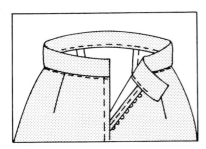

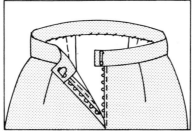

4. Alternatively the 'stitch-in-the-ditch' method can be used to attach the second edge from the right side of the garment.

5. Hooks and bars, or button and buttonhole complete the waistband.

16 HEMS

There are so many ways of stitching hems, and you need to make different decisions for different fabrics.

The first criteria is to get the garment to the length you require, and, because of the different ways in which people stand, it is vital that the hem should be levelled *from the floor* upwards.

You will need help with this job, and either the helper will have to kneel on the ground, or you will have to stand on something higher.

A bean-stick with a rubber band round it can prove to be an ideal guide to the length required, always checked from the ground *up* and not from the waist down. Stand the stick upright on the ground and put a pin horizontally into the fabric at the required length. Continue around the gar-ment placing pins at regular, fairly close intervals. Next take out the pins as you stitch a tacking line where the pins were placed, whilst you are doing this you should watch that the hem is taking a good line on the fabric. You should now trim the hem to the amount you want to leave turned up, and this will vary with the fabric, and the amount of width in the skirt.

If you are not a good hand sewer, or the fabric is so fine that the hem is going to show, I can see no reason for not machining the hem – especially if you have special stitches on your machine.

The finish of the top of the turned hem must also be a consideration (the zig–zag machine stitch is really useful here) and you can use any method described in the seam-finishing techniques.

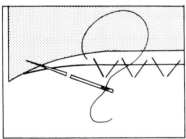

1. Slip-stitching can be used for both woven and stretch fabrics and is particularly recommended because you can control so easily the degree of tightness that you require from the stitching. The stitching is done slightly underneath the top of the turned hem and is therefore not seen when completed.

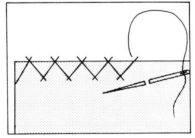

2. Herringbone stitch both neatens and secures a hem, and is most often used for heavier fabrics and for those that fray easily.

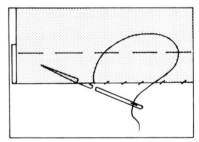

3. Catch stitch is a useful method for secure hems, and is often used when the top edge of the hem has been turned under for neatening.

A 5 cm (2 in) hem is normal for many garments, but a smaller hem will be required for flared skirts, if you are to avoid excessive pleating in the turned hem.

Remember that jersey and stretch fabrics must be stitched loosely so that the hem will also stretch.

17 SLEEVES

Sleeves form an important part in the creation of fashion. Often a change of sleeve can completely alter the 'look' of a garment, and a quick look at a book on the history of costume will soon illustrate to you what an important part sleeves have played in the styles down the centuries.

You can, of course, just join two pieces of fabric that will fit your hips and bust and leave two holes at the sides to put your arms through, and an opening for your head, rather like today's T-shirts.

However the 'set-in' sleeve, which fits closer to the body shape plays a big part in today's dressmaking. Usually the sleeve 'head' is bigger than the armhole, and this means the sleeve has to be eased with gentle gathering to make it fit.

In the modern factory, and particularly with knitted fabrics, where they are making up garments with special safety-overlock machines, the sleeve and the armhole are the same size, with no ease allowed.

Shoulder pads can affect the way a sleeve looks, and indeed the way the bodice of a garment hangs, so it is useful to have a set in your workbox so that you can try your garment with and without them in.

Remember that fabrics with a man-made-fibre content will not allow you to press and shrink away any excess fullness, so do not cut out with too much gather on a sleeve head, unless it is meant to be a gathered sleeve.

If you practise with the small-scale sleeve patterns from this book you should be able to create your own sleeve designs, and you could then follow the changing fashions without buying new patterns.

I would also recommend that you work with *two* sleeves patterns, one for each side, in case you have to cut from fabric that is not folded. This way you will not end up with two sleeves for the same side, as the front and back of a sleeve are cut differently and must not be reversed if you want a good fit.

Method 1

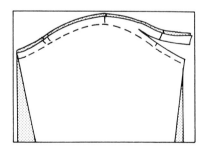 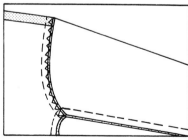

1. Matching the front and back notches on both the sleeve and the bodice of the garment, tack and stitch the sleeve into the armhole before stitching the side seams. Trim the seam and neaten the seam edges.

2. Stitch the side seam of the garment, and the sleeve seam in one operation.

Method 2

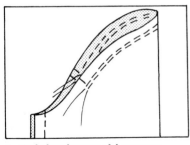

1. With the side seams of the garment stitched and the sleeve seam stitched, measure the size of the armhole and gather the sleeve-head to fit, distributing the gathers between the front and back notches.

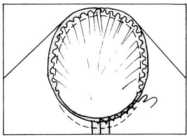

2. Pin, tack, and stitch the sleeve into the armhole.

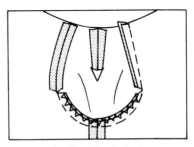

3. Neaten the seams by stitching together and zig-zagging the edge.

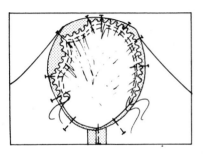

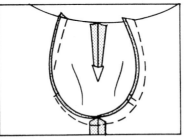

4. When a lot of gather is involved the sleeve should be pinned into the armhole in sections, and each section gathered evenly to produce the best results.

5. The sleeve is always machined into the armhole from the sleeve side so that you can keep control of the gathers under the machine foot.

Method 3

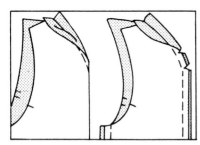

1. Raglan and kimono sleeves can either be cut in one piece with a dart in the shoulders, or in two complete sections with a centre top seam.
The dart, or the seam must first be stitched.

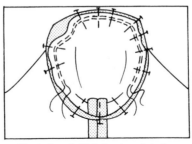

2. With the side seam of the garment stitched and pressed the sleeve is then stitched into the armhole.

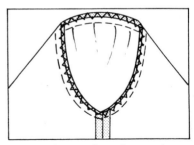

3. A smoother fit will be obtained, particularly at the neckline if the underarm seam is neatened with the edges together, and the two sides of the sleeve have pressed open seams.

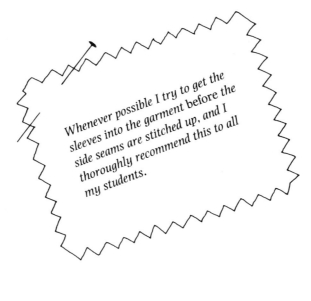

18 GATHERS AND FRILLS

It is quite astounding how often the process of gathering is used in the making of clothes, and it appears in many different disguises.

Very often the instructions are for one longer edge to be gathered to fit a shorter edge, this can be just to 'ease' two pieces together, with very little obvious gather, or it can be to form a frilled effect, which requires a lot of gather – dependent upon the weight of fabric and the amount of gather you require. The amount of 'excess fabric' that becomes a gather can also be dealt with in several other ways, so that the long edge could be pintucked or smocked, or even shirred or pleated, and you should bear these alternatives in mind whenever you see gathers mentioned in a pattern.

Very effective skirts can be made by having two tiers of fabric – the top tier being one and a half times your waist size, the bottom tier being gathered to the top tier, and, with an elasticated waist and a machined hem you have one of the simplest garments possible to make.

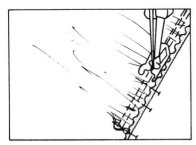

1. Stitch gathering threads into the edge of fabric to be gathered.

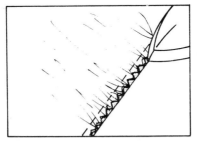

2. Pin the edge to be gathered into the required position on the other fabric edge, at the ends only.

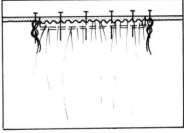

3. Gently gather the fabric up, using spacing pins, to ensure even gathering along the distance.

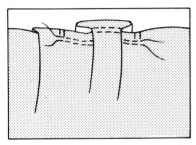

4. You can usually machine over horizontally placed pins, taking them out as the machine foot reaches each pin. Otherwise tack the edges before machining. Always machine from the gathered side to control the gathers.

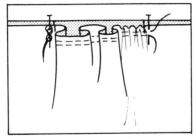

5. Trim and neaten the seam, and then gently press the seam only as you do not want to press pleats into the gathers of the garment.

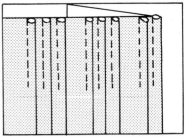

6. This diagram illustrates how you could have pin-tucked the gathering distance if preferred.

Frills

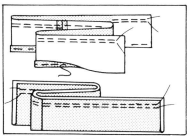

7. Single fabric frills should preferably be cut on the cross of the fabric, one edge is hemmed and the gathering threads stitched into the remaining edge. You will most often require twice the length of the finished length to achieve a successful gathered effect. Double frills are prepared by folding the fabric and stitching gathering threads into the remaining edges.

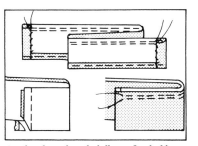

8. The edges of single frills are finished by neat seams, and by stitching and turning the ends of double frills.

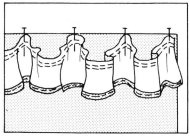

9. Pin the edge to be frilled at either end, then at regular intervals along the piece.

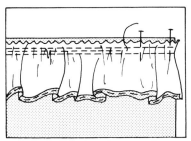

10. Pull up the gathers, between each pin, to achieve an even finish. Tack and machine the frill.

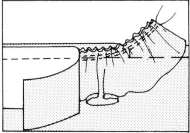

11. Once the frill is the required length it could be attached to, say, a neckline, using a binding strip to fold over the edges.

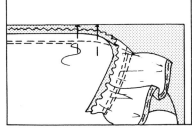

12. If the frill is to be 'sandwiched' between two fabrics pin and tack the pieces together, as illustrated before machining.

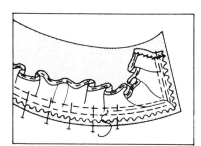

13. Turning corners with frilling is very much easier if the frill has been cut on the cross of the fabric.

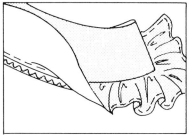

14. The attached frill can either have the seam line neatened for the inside of a garment or it can be 'sandwiched' between two pieces, as in a cuff or collar edge.

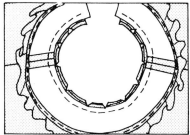

15. Frilling in a neckline can be attached exactly as a collar, with the facing stitched on afterwards.

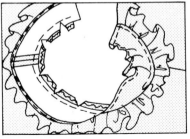

16. *Turn the facing to the inside exactly as in the collar technique.*

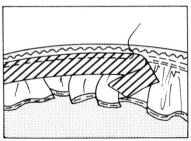

17. *Frilling can be attached with bought bias binding by stitching one edge of the binding to cover the frill.*

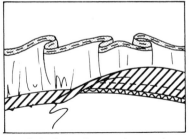

18. *The binding is then turned over to the inside of the garment and stitched over the seam.*

Gathered strips are used to produce frills between two fabric edges, and pretty trimming, gathered, can make a successful collar.

19 POCKETS AND FLAPS

Whether you need a pocket in which to keep 'bits and pieces' or whether you just want to decorate a garment, making pockets can transform the very plain into something special.

You can make pockets from contrast fabric, or from fabric cut in a different direction from the rest of the garment.

The *patch* pocket can be exactly that . . . a pocket which patches up a hole, and you should look in the shops at the unexpected places (like trouser legs and sleeves) where the addition of a pocket has transformed the outfit intentionally.

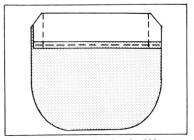

1. The simplest type of pocket should have a folded edge at the top and can be either square or round cornered. Hem the top edge, and then fold it to the right side of the fabric and machine the top edges.

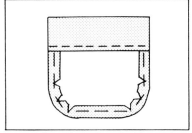

2. Turn the pocket to the right side and clip the seams before turning and tacking them into place.

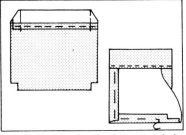

3. The same procedure for the top is applied to the square pocket, but it will help to turn the square bottom corners if you trim these as illustrated.

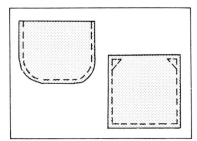

4. Once turned and pressed the pockets can be top stitched to the garment. The reinforced machining at the top corners is recommended to avoid the pocket breaking away from the garment in use.

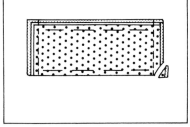

5. To prepare a pocket flap you are advised to use interfacing to keep it crisp and to support any buttonhole that might be used. Check the length required with the top of the pocket, then stitch the two short ends of the flap.

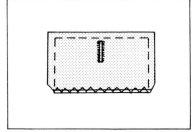

6. Turn the flap to the right side, neaten the raw edges, and put in the buttonhole, if required.

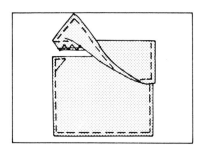

7. Stitch the flap above the pocket, as illustrated.

Easy Fully Lined Method

Cut the pocket fabric approx 5 cms (2 ins) longer
than required, and the lining approx 2.5 cms (1 in)
shorter than required.

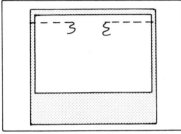

1. Stitch the lining to one edge of the fabric.

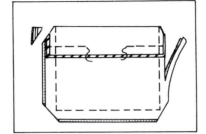

2. Stitch the lining to the other edge of the fabric leaving a gap unstitched in the middle.
Fold the pocket as illustrated and stitch the side seams.
Clip and trim the seams.

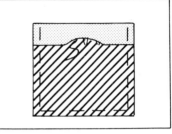

3. Turn the pocket to the right side, through the unstitched gap left in step 2. Press and hand stitch the gap.

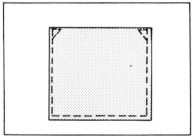

4. Stitch the pocket to the garment, reinforce-stitch the corners.

You can embroider designs, either by hand or machine, and you can transform an old garment merely by putting on pocket flaps, and matching them to cuffs, collar, machining stitching, or piping.

20 DEALING WITH 'V' NECKLINES

It is always easier if there is a centre front seam on both the garment and the facing, and both facings and collars should be stitched to the neckline *before* the centre front seam is done.

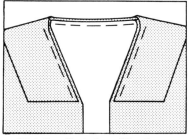 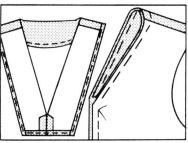 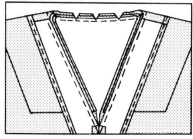

1. Stitch the collar to the neckline, then stitch the facings to the neckline, making sure that you leave the seam allowance for the centre front unstitched on both the facing and the garment.

2. Stitch the centre-front garment seam and the centre-front facings seam.

3. Press both seams open, then complete the stitching of the neckline at the base of the 'V'.

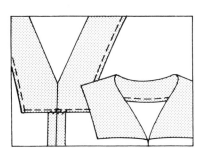

4. Trim, clip, and layer the seams and turn the facings to the inside of the garment.

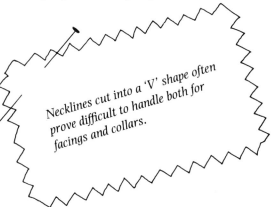

Necklines cut into a 'V' shape often prove difficult to handle both for facings and collars.

THE FINISHING TOUCH

Whenever you stitch an open seam you have to think about the raw edges of the fabric that are left on the inside of the garment.

BUTTONS AND BUTTONHOLES

These seem to crop up in practically every type of garment at some time or other.

Bound buttonholes require practice, and a good control of both fabric and machine.

Handworked buttonholes are not too difficult, and most people who enjoy embroidery would find them very easy indeed.

However, today's machines usually have a buttonhole facility, some easier to use than others, but all requiring practice, particularly on whatever fabric you are proposing to use.

Buttonholes can go either up and down or across the centre front line of a front fastening garment.

The up and down method is generally used when a front band is part of the design.

When the across method is used *one* third of the buttonhole should be over the centre front line.

Always buy the buttons first. Try to match the size to the distance they must cover, and also to their suitability with the fabric. Err on the small side with buttons rather than buy them too big.

Buttons with two holes do not spread the buttonhole open as much as a button with four holes.

On jackets and heavier garments *always* use backing buttons, which look more professional and stop buttons coming off.

Do not sew buttons too tightly to the flat fabric, a thread shank, worked when the button is sewn, will give a smoother look when the garment is fastened.

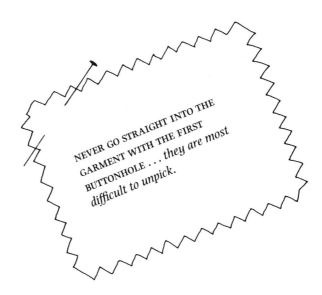

NEVER GO STRAIGHT INTO THE GARMENT WITH THE FIRST BUTTONHOLE . . . *they are most difficult to unpick.*

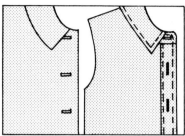

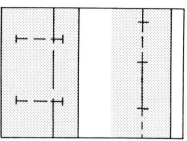

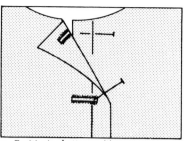

1. Buttonholes going up and down in a banded front, and across in other types of garment.

2. Buttonhole positioning across a centre front line, or up and down a banded front centre line.

3. Positioning button position on across buttonholes.

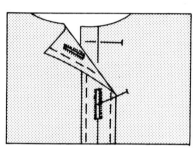

4. Position of buttons on up and down buttonholes.

PIN TUCKS

A very attractive effect can be created by making the garment with a section of the pattern using fabric that has been pin tucked.

Pin Tucking is simply a very small seam allowance stitched into the fabric at regular intervals, and the small tucks created are then pressed in the direction required on the right side of the garment.

I have always found it much easier if the fabric is pin tucked across a straight piece of fabric, and the pattern pieces cut out after this has been done.

Pin tucks can often replace gathers or darts, and they look particularly good on the back of a blouse, where the body section is normally gathered to fit the yoke.

BELTS AND BELT LOOPS

A change of belt, both the type and the colour, can completely transform an outfit, and you should experiment with different textures and shades.

If a belt is to be tied, either in a knot or a bow, it will look and handle very much better if the fabric is cut on the cross. Loops to carry the belt can be made from matching fabric, or you can make them by hand.

PLEATS

Pleats play an important role in dressmaking, both for styling and effect.

Taking the hips into the waist size on skirts and trousers can be done with darts, but it looks good (particularly on the front of a garment) if the dart is used as a pleat, which opens gently as you move and sit down.

Three times your waistsize of fabric can be pleated to fit a waistband and will make an excellent skirt. These pleats are sometimes stitched part way down from the waist to keep them in place.

CASINGS

The word 'casing' is used in dressmaking to describe the hem, or the additional fabric that is stitched to carry either elastic or a cord which can be tied.

An easy skirt can be made with an elasticated top hem, and the turned hem on an anorak can carry the cord fastening.

If a waistline is to be elasticated on a dress it is possible to stitch fabric either to the right or wrong side, through which elastic can be threaded.

If you do decide to elasticate a waist always stitch the casing slightly below your natural waistline, to allow for the pouched effect that it requires.

BANDS

The 'band effect' can be obtained in several different ways: wide trimming can be stitched to the edges of a jacket; facings can be brought to the right side of the garment and top stitched into place; roll collars, in contrast fabric can be used, or you could knit a collar to stitch on to a garment.

In stretch fabrics bands for the neckline and sleeves can be cut in contrast fabric.

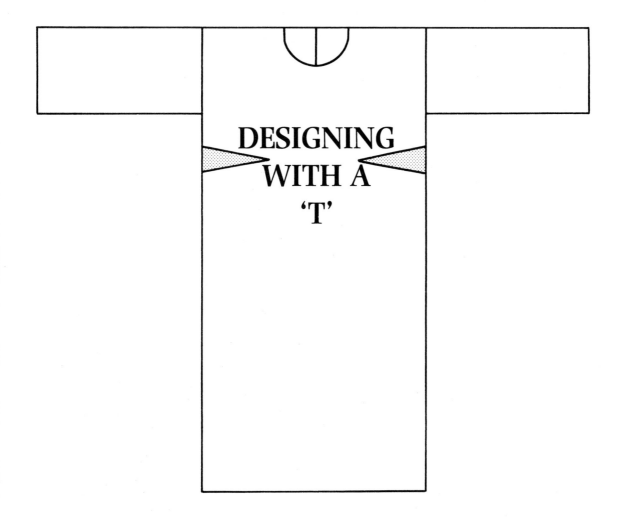

DESIGNING WITH A 'T'

SIMPLE 'STARTER' PATTERN

All measurements are in centimetres

RECOMMENDED FOR KNITTED FABRICS ONLY

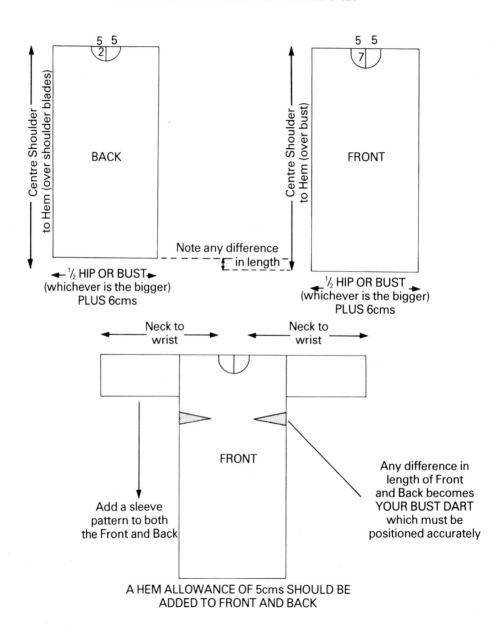

BACK

5 5

2

Centre Shoulder to Hem (over shoulder blades)

← ½ HIP OR BUST →
(whichever is the bigger)
PLUS 6cms

Note any difference in length

FRONT

5 5

7

Centre Shoulder to Hem (over bust)

½ HIP OR BUST
(whichever is the bigger)
PLUS 6cms

Neck to wrist   Neck to wrist

FRONT

Add a sleeve pattern to both the Front and Back

Any difference in length of Front and Back becomes YOUR BUST DART which must be positioned accurately

A HEM ALLOWANCE OF 5cms SHOULD BE ADDED TO FRONT AND BACK

DESIGNING ON A 'T'

A simple T-shape can change into a whole spectrum of ideas, both for outline and colour co-ordination or contrast.

If you have never made clothes before, now is your opportunity to make something really simple.

THE PATTERNS

Recommended for *knitted* fabrics only, when there is no front or back opening used in the design.

A centre front or centre back seam can be added to the pattern if required.

Woven fabrics can be used if the opening is long enough to allow you to get into the garment easily.

The angle of the side bust dart can be changed to slope gently upwards from the outer edge.

If you do this you should fold out the dart in the new position and adjust the line of the side seam to take account of the changed angle.

The combined body and sleeve pattern can be treated as a jig saw, which can be cut up, and reassembled in any way.

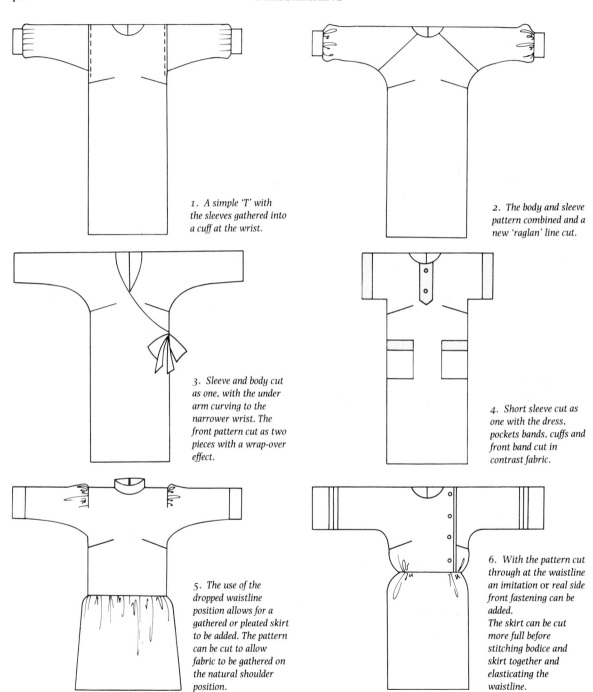

1. A simple 'T' with
the sleeves gathered into
a cuff at the wrist.

2. The body and sleeve
pattern combined and a
new 'raglan' line cut.

3. Sleeve and body cut
as one, with the under
arm curving to the
narrower wrist. The
front pattern cut as two
pieces with a wrap-over
effect.

4. Short sleeve cut as
one with the dress,
pockets bands, cuffs and
front band cut in
contrast fabric.

5. The use of the
dropped waistline
position allows for a
gathered or pleated skirt
to be added. The pattern
can be cut to allow
fabric to be gathered on
the natural shoulder
position.

6. With the pattern cut
through at the waistline
an imitation or real side
front fastening can be
added.
The skirt can be cut
more full before
stitching bodice and
skirt together and
elasticating the
waistline.

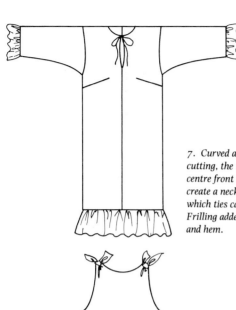

7. *Curved armhole cutting, the use of a centre front seam to create a neck opening to which ties can be added. Frilling added to wrists and hem.*

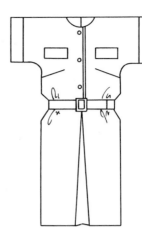

8. *Using the waistline position a centre front pleat can be introduced into the skirt, and a centre button fastening to the bodice. Pocket flaps and contrast sleeve bands add interest.*

9. *Scoop the armholes back onto the shoulder, and lower the neckline. Side seams are flared for extra width.*

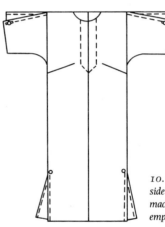

10. *Slashed sleeves and side split skirt, can be machine top-stitched for emphasis.*

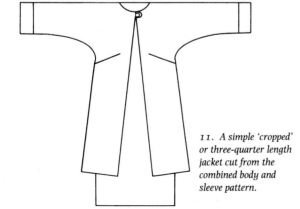

11. *A simple 'cropped' or three-quarter length jacket cut from the combined body and sleeve pattern.*

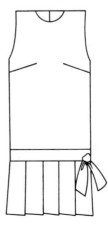

12. *Cut-away armholes, bottom skirt taken off at any level and pleated, with a crossway cut band set in between the skirt and top before stitching.*

ABBREVIATIONS

alt.	=	alternate
approx.	=	approximately
beg.	=	beginning
cm	=	centimetre(s)
cont.	=	continue
dec.	=	decrease
foll.	=	following
gm	=	gram(s)
g.st.	=	garter stitch (i.e. every row K)
in	=	inch(es)
inc.	=	increase
K	=	knit
P	=	purl
rem.	=	remaining
rep.	=	repeat
rev.st.st.	=	reverse side of stocking stitch
sl.	=	slip
st(s).	=	stitch(es)
st.st.	=	stocking stitch
tbl	=	through back of loop (i.e. through the back of the stitch)
tog	=	together
tog tbl	=	together through back of loop
yon	=	yarn over needle

KNITTING

INTRODUCTION

This section of the book is designed to help knitters in three ways. If you are a new knitter, I hope that you will begin at the beginning and work your way through, so that you develop and learn new techniques, tips and hints as you go along.

For the more experienced knitter, this section is a reference for all the little ideas and additions that make the craft more satisfying than ever, as well as being a source of information to take you further into the whole business of knitting. It also includes twelve fashion garment patterns for you to choose from, and there is a great variety here to appeal to all.

Using either the book, or book and programme together, we progress from the very simple to the complex, collecting ideas all along the way, and helping and correcting with the inevitable, but hopefully only occasional, problems – some very common, some downright odd! Above all, I hope to convince newcomers how enjoyable and satisfying knitting is, perhaps even converting a few sceptics, of whichever sex, to its charms, and to help those of you who already know how, to have the whole craft, 'All Stitched Up'.

Joy Gammon

KNITTING NEEDLE SIZES

Metric Size

2 mm	$2\frac{1}{4}$ mm	$2\frac{1}{2}$ mm	$2\frac{3}{4}$ mm	3 mm	$3\frac{1}{4}$ mm	$3\frac{1}{2}$ mm	$3\frac{3}{4}$ mm	4 mm	$4\frac{1}{2}$ mm

English Size

14	13	—	12	11	10	—	9	8	7

5 mm	$5\frac{1}{2}$ mm	6 mm	$6\frac{1}{2}$ mm	7 mm	$7\frac{1}{2}$ mm	8 mm	9 mm	10 mm	12 mm
6	5	4	3	2	1	0	00	000	0000

KNITTING TODAY

CHOOSING YARN

The first exciting step in the process of making a knitted garment is, of course, choosing a yarn. This is more complicated, and more fun, than it used to be because there are so many, but this variety means that you have a greater opportunity of choosing exactly what you want. As well as liking the yarn, and being inspired to knit with it, it is worth checking what fibres it is made from, and how well they wash and wear, so that you can choose a yarn appropriate to the garment which you plan to make. Think about weight and thickness too, there are lots of summer yarns these days, not just winter woolies, so you can knit for all the year round.

If you are a beginner, go for speed! Thickish, smooth or slubbed yarns are best, with some colour interest so that the fabric is varied even if your knitting is a bit basic. Very fine yarns are for the experienced or dedicated, and bouclé loops and very fluffy yarns can cause problems, if only because it is difficult to see where you are and what you have done. Brushed fluffy yarns are very difficult to undo if mistakes need correcting.

If you can, knit up a small square in your chosen yarn before you buy, to give you the feel of the yarn and to check that you like the finished fabric before you commit yourself.

CHOOSING NEEDLES

To a large extent the *yarn* will choose the size of

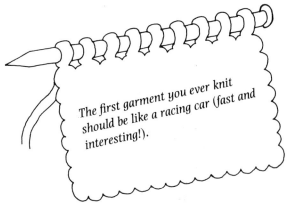

The first garment you ever knit should be like a racing car (fast and interesting!).

the needles, in that a needle will probably be recommended on the ball band, or by your wool shop. You can of course vary the needle size as much as you like, and may need to do so in order to achieve the right tension. (See section on tension which follows.) With the sort of medium thick yarn which a beginner might choose, very fine needles would be difficult, but, surprisingly, very thick needles are quite difficult to handle too, and a medium needle is best to start with.

Needles are most frequently made from metal and these are strong and pleasant to use, but they can also be plastic which are light and attractive, especially for children (but do be careful that they do not break). Some old needles are made of bone or wood, and wooden needles can still be bought today, as can bamboo. These all feel good and are light and warm to use.

Don't go for very big needles to start with. They are tempting but more difficult than they look.

Needle Type	Uses	
Straight	Conventional knitting.	
Double ended	Working in the round.	Very versatile, can be used for any number of stitches. A tricky technique for a beginner.
Circular	Working in the round.	Very versatile and quick to use. Need several lengths in each size for varying numbers of stitches.

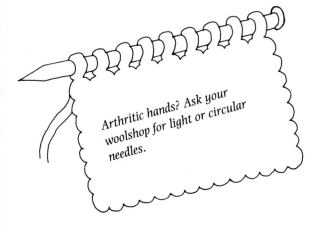

Arthritic hands? Ask your woolshop for light or circular needles.

NEEDLE GAUGES

All that is really necessary for knitting is yarn and needles, but I will mention other useful bits of equipment as we come to garments in the book where they might be needed. The only other useful extra at this stage is a needle gauge, especially if you have a fuddle of needles that were Granny's or Mum's and half are old sizes and half no sizes at all. Then a simple plastic gauge sorts these out, and also any unmarked circular or double-ended needles.

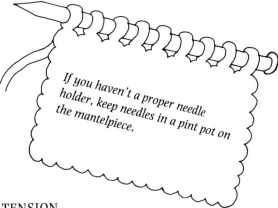

If you haven't a proper needle holder, keep needles in a pint pot on the mantelpiece.

TENSION

Having chosen your yarn and needles, you only need one other thing before you begin a garment. You need to know how many stitches to the inch *you* knit, in your chosen yarn and stitch pattern. To do this, knit a square large enough to measure at least 4 ins across, and then measure how many stitches per inch you have.

If you are trying to match a tension given in a pattern, cast on more stitches than the pattern suggests will be necessary for the usual 4 in (10 cm) square, and work more rows than recommended in the stitch pattern given, usually in stocking stitch. Flatten, but do not stretch the knitting, and place pins to mark the number of stitches and rows that the tension recommends. (*1 and 2*)

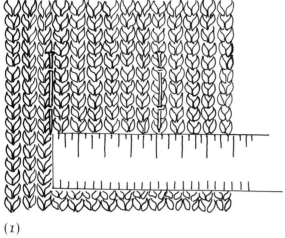

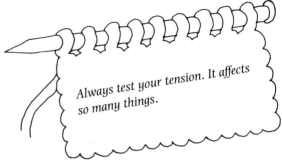

Always test your tension. It affects so many things.

(1)

Choosing stitch size in knitting is just like choosing wall-tile size in DIY: if the tiles are wrong they will overlap the bathroom door or leave nasty gaps round the mirror. If the stitches are wrong, the jumper may strangle or swamp you, or turn into a bolero or a frock! And wrong tension can make a knitted fabric floppy, stand up on its own, or one that washes and wears badly.

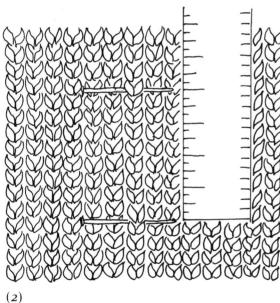

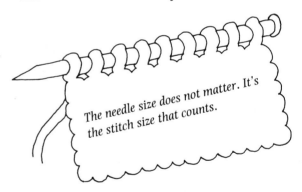

The needle size does not matter. It's the stitch size that counts.

(2)

If your measurements between the pins are greater than 4 ins (10 cms), your tension is loose, (that is, the stitches are too big) so change to a smaller needle; if your measurements are less than 4 ins your tension is tight (that is, the stitches are too small) so change to a larger needle and try again.

Use tension to avoid problems. Some people *knit* more loosely than they *purl* (or vice versa), creating a ridged effect with stocking stitch. If this is very noticeable, use odd needles to correct it, one larger than the other: and, if leaving your knitting for a long time, leave it on a smaller needle to avoid stretching one row, and try not to knit half of a row and leave it. Always finish the row.

If, in spite of all this, your tension is still variable, make a virtue out of a necessity and knit a fashionable jumper in one of the knobbly, slubby yarns that are so uneven anyway that no one will notice the odd inconsistency from you.

GARMENTS FROM SQUARES

Because knitting is so squashy, very simple shapes make very satisfying garments. The most simple shape of all being a square. To make the garment in the drawing, on page 81, count how many stitches to the inch your chosen yarn, needles and stitch pattern give you (see tension page 77), and multiply this by the number of inches wide the garment is to be. This is the number of stitches to cast on.

Get someone else to cast on for you if you are a total beginner.

Don't worry if your casting on looks too small. It always does.

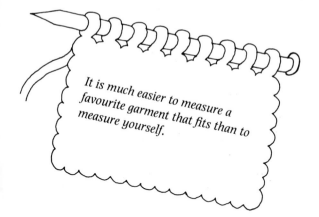

It is much easier to measure a favourite garment that fits than to measure yourself.

Work in your chosen stitch pattern until the work is long enough. Garter stitch (every row knit), is the most simple stitch of all, and makes this garment as easy as the blanket squares and dishcloths which we all made at school. Also, garter stitch does not curl up which is essential for this top as there are no arm and neck bands, so the edges need to lie flat.

CASTING ON

There are many ways of casting on. Choose the ones you like best, and don't panic if the cast-on stitches don't look wide enough. They never do. Trust your judgement and your sums and you will find all is well by the time you have knitted a little.

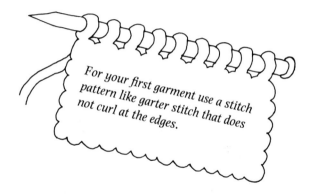

For your first garment use a stitch pattern like garter stitch that does not curl at the edges.

CASTING OFF

When the square is the length you want it to be, simply cast off. Make sure that you do this loosely, so that the square isn't gathered at the top.

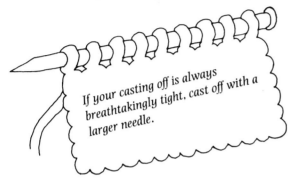

If your casting off is always breathtakingly tight, cast off with a larger needle.

Carefully sew shoulder (be sure to leave a wide neck opening) and side seams. (See Making Up, page 86) and your simple top is complete!

If in doubt, get someone to show you.

This kind of top is terrific in a very exciting yarn, or in silly colours; in a stringy yarn on huge needles, or in furry yarn cut off very short. It makes a lovely cotton beach cover-up when made very long and slit up the sides. Or why not leave it un-seamed and lace or tie it together?

ADDING A WELT

The garment in the photograph has a welt; a band of rib at the beginning, which is the most simple kind of shaping to add to a garment. Usually worked on needles two sizes smaller than the ones chosen for the main stitch, welts are ribbed by working alternate stitches in knit and purl, then, on the next row, working the stitch in the opposite way, that is, all stitches knitted on the previous row are purled, and vice versa. This zig-zags the work and gives it 'stretch'.

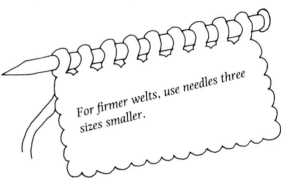

For firmer welts, use needles three sizes smaller.

'SQUARE'

This pattern is for a simple square garment with a welt, using the ideas discussed so far, and in an interesting fashion yarn. Use it as it is, or adapt it to your own size and ideas.

Materials

Wendy Monet in Lilac mix. 4 (4, 4) × 100 gm balls. 1 pr. 6 mm (No. 4) needles. 1 pr 5 mm (No. 6) needles. (Or alter to suit your tension if required.)

Tension

13 sts and 24 rows = 4 ins (10 cms) on 6 mm (No. 4) needles in garter stitch.

Sizes

To fit 30–32 (34–36, 38–40) ins.

Back and Front (both alike)

Using needles two sizes smaller than those chosen for main tension, e.g. 5 mm (No. 6), cast on 55 (61, 69) sts and work 2½ ins in K1, P1 rib, beginning and ending every row K and keeping rib correct in between. Change to needles chosen for main tension, e.g. 6 mm (No. 4) and work in garter st. (every row K), to a total measurement of 21 (22, 23) ins measured flat and unstretched. Cast off loosely.

Making Up

Do not press. Oversew, as neatly as possible, shoulder and side seams, leaving a 10 (11, 11) in neck opening and 8 (9, 9½) in armholes.

STOCKING STITCH

This is the familiar smooth knitted fabric achieved on two needles by working alternate rows of knit and purl. It gives a lovely texture in complex yarns and, in plain yarns, has that satisfying clean look because all of the bumps, mistakes and colour changes are thrown on to the wrong side.

Stripes are the easiest pattern to knit and look really good in stocking stitch. Have fun with colour, arranging it beforehand so that the stripes occur where you want them, and vary stripe width as much as you like. To avoid lots of joins, work an even number of rows in every stripe and, if you will need a colour again, carry it loosely up the side, weaving it into the end stitches occasionally, until it is required.

'Square'

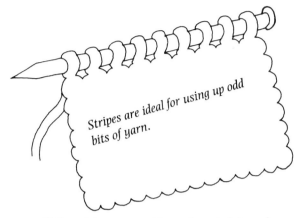

Stripes are ideal for using up odd bits of yarn.

If the stripes are wide and varied in colour so that it is necessary to break off yarns and join in new ones, join by weaving in rather than by knotting which is messy, or darning in later with a needle, which takes ages. To weave in, at about eight stitches before the end of the last row of a stripe, begin to weave in the end of the new yarn, and weave it into the end of the row, in just the same way as in Fair Isle knitting. (See the drawing on page 122.) Then, at the beginning of the next row, weave in the tail end of the last colour in the same way. The job is done then, neatly and firmly with no more work at the making-up stage.

If you don't fasten off yarn ends on a stripe pattern, leave them as a fringe.

SIZE AND MEASUREMENT

The basic measurements needed for knitting are chest size, usually plus 2 inches of ease for a comfortable fit (half of this is the measurement across the garment of course), and the underarm measurement, that is the measurement of the underarm seam. If you are designing your own patterns or adapting other patterns, you also need to know the neck opening width and depth and armhole depth. Again it is much easier to measure an actual garment than to measure yourself, especially on your own. Length, obviously, is whatever you want it. (3)

The most simple armhole shaping is a dropped armhole or sleeve, that is, one with no shaping at all, as on these first four garments, and the most usual neck shaping is a round neck.

ROUND NECK SHAPING

The slash neck on the first garment had no shaping at all. It was just a wide enough slit to sit comfortably around a neck, but a fitted round neck needs to be shaped on the garment front. About half of the stitches which will make the neck are left on a holder at the centre of the work, then the remaining stitches at each side are decreased from the neck edge to give a rounded slope. Unused stitches can be left on a spare needle, although this does get in the way and can fall out. Stitch holders, resembling giant safety pins, are best, or for small numbers of stitches use ordinary safety pins (nappy pins are ideal).

DECREASING

Decreasing is done by working two stitches together, usually knitting them, and is written as K2tog. (4)

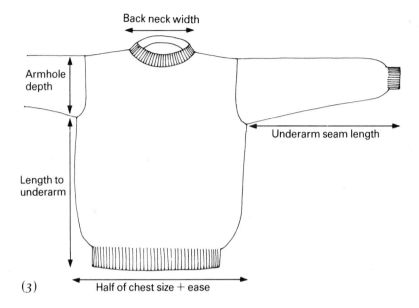

(3)

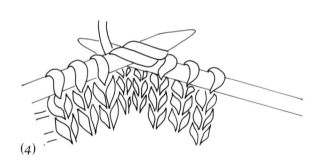

(4)

(5)

This creates a stitch sloping to the right, which will be virtually invisible at the right-hand end of a knit row. Some patterns need to work two stitches together with a stitch which slopes to the left and is therefore hidden at the left-hand end of a knit row. This is done by knitting two together through the *back* of the loops of the stitches and is written as K2tog.tbl. (5)

These decreases may be paired, or worked several stitches in, especially on Raglan shaping for a decorative effect.

For a lacy decreasing, lose 2 sts instead of one, and replace one of them with 'yarn over needle'.

PICKING UP FOR BANDS OF RIB

Many people find this difficult, and perhaps do it less well than they might, and are then dissatisfied with the result. Here are some ideas to make it easier and more successful.

Patterns usually give an order in which stitches should be picked up for bands of rib, and also say that stitches should be picked up and knitted at the same time. Instead of this, pick up in reverse order, with the opposite side facing, starting at the other end, using a very small needle and without knitting the stitches. This is much easier, and the stitches can then be knitted off the needle and mistakes corrected as you go along, as well as any adjustment of the stitch numbers, where these are wrong or uneven.

Mark out long edges to be picked up in sections with pins, perhaps halves and quarters or even inches, dividing the stitches evenly throughout the sections so that they don't all end up at one end.

If you find you have picked up too many or, more usually, too few stitches, distribute the additional numbers needed throughout the work to keep it even. Knit into the *back* of picked-up loops, especially loose ones, to avoid holes.

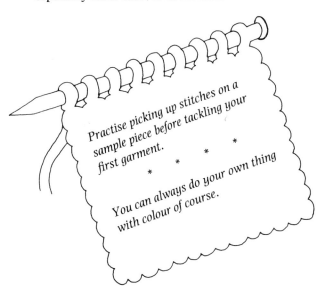

Practise picking up stitches on a sample piece before tackling your first garment.

*   *   *

You can always do your own thing with colour of course.

'MATELOT'

This pattern is similar to the previous garment made of plain squares but includes all the new techniques we have just covered: stripes, neck shaping (to give a generous, casual round neck), and picking up (to knit ribs).

Materials

Patons Diploma Double Knitting. Main Colour (Royal blue) 5(5,5,6,6,6) × 50 gm balls. Contrast (White) 3(4,4,4,5) × 50 gm balls. 1 pr. 4 mm (No. 8) needles. 1 pr. 3¼ mm (No. 10) needles. (Or alter to suit your tension if required.)

Tension

24 sts and 32 rows = 4 ins (10 cms) in st.st. on 4 mm (No. 8) needles.

Sizes

To fit 34(36,38,40,42,44) ins with 3 ins of ease.

Back

Using needles two sizes smaller than those chosen for main tension, e.g. 3¼ mm (No. 10), cast on 111(117,123,129,135,141) sts in main colour, and work 2(2,2½,2½,2½,2½) ins in K1,P1 rib, beginning and ending every row K and keeping rib correct in between. Change to needles chosen for main tension, e.g. 4 mm (No. 8), and st.st. beg. K and stripe pattern: 8 rows contrast, 8 rows main colour, repeated throughout.* Work straight in stripe pattern to a total measurement of 23(23,23,23½,24½,24½) ins, ending with the last row of a stripe, which will be a P row.
Next row (Using same colour as on previous row), cast off 31(34,37,39,40,42) sts, K until 31(34,37,39,40,42) sts rem, place the 49(49,49,51,55,57) sts just worked on to a holder, cast off to end.

Front

Work as given for Back as far as *.

Work straight in stripe pattern to a total measurement of 19(19,19,19½,20½,20½) ins ending with the last row of a stripe, which will be a P row.

Next row (To shape neck) Keeping stripe pattern correct, K43(46,49,52,54,56) sts, turn, and work this side first.

**Dec. I st. at neck edge on next 6(6,6,7,8,8) rows, then on every alt. row 6 times. (31,34,37,39,40,42 sts rem.)

Work straight, still in stripe pattern, until front matches back at armhole edge, so ending with a P row and the last row of a stripe.

Cast off in the same colour as the previous row.**

Place centre 25(25,25,25,27,29) sts on a holder.

Rejoin yarn to rem. sts and K to end. Rep. from ** to **.

Neckband

Using matching colour and back stitch, join left shoulder seam.

With smaller needles, main colour and right side facing, pick up and K the 49(49,49,51,55,57) sts from the back neck holder, working 2tog. in the middle; 29(29,33,35,35,35) sts down the left front slope; the 25(25,25,25,27,29) sts from the front neck holder, and 29(29,33,35,35,35) sts up the right front neck. (131,131,139,145,151,155 sts.) Work 10 rows in K1,P1 rib in the same way as for the back. Cast off loosely in rib.

Armbands

Mark a point on the armhole edge of the back and the front 9(9,9½,9½,10,10) ins down from the shoulder seam, i.e. 9(9,9½,9½,10,10) stripes down from the shoulder seam.

Between the two points, with the right side facing, using main colour and smaller needles, pick up and K, at the rate of approximately 6 sts per inch, i.e. 6 sts per stripe, 109(109,113,113,119,119) sts. Work 10 rows in K1,P1 rib in the same way as for the back. Cast off loosely in rib.

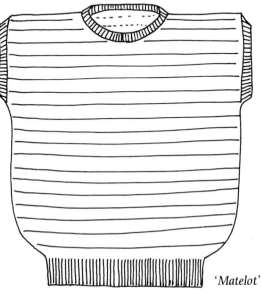

'Matelot'

Making Up (See notes on making up which follow)

Do not press. Make up rem. seams in back stitch as carefully as possible matching stripes.

MAKING UP

Each row of the welt ribs on the Matelot pattern begins and ends with a K st. This gives a neater edge for making up, and anything that helps with making up has got to be a good idea. Here are some more.

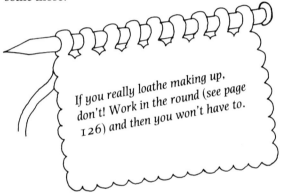

If you really loathe making up, don't! Work in the round (see page 126) and then you won't have to.

If in doubt, don't press, especially acrylic yarns. If you do press, follow ball band instructions or ask at your wool shop for advice first.

Before you press, block your work, that is spread the pieces out flat (a carpeted floor is ideal), and pin them out to the measurements that the piece should be. I'm not sure that it does the carpet underlay any good, but what the eye doesn't see . . .!

If you must press, use a pressing cloth. Better still, lightly spray the pieces with water from a fine plant spray (preferably having washed out the greenfly pong first), then allow the knitting to dry where it is. It is surprising how successful this is.

Use glass-headed pins to pin the pieces together, they don't get so easily lost. Pin ends first, then the middle, then middles again for an even match.

Sew up with a tapestry needle (a sharp needle splits the yarn and makes sewing difficult), and, if the yarn is very fluffy or slubby, or it's a thick fashion yarn, use a matching smooth thin yarn – it's much easier.

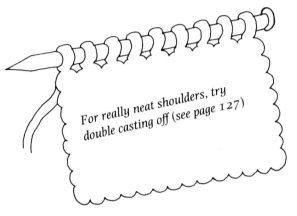

For really neat shoulders, try double casting off (see page 127)

Try to sew up colour patterns with the self colour, and carefully match patterns and shapings for a neat finish.

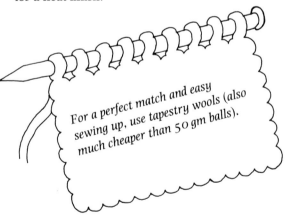

For a perfect match and easy sewing up, use tapestry wools (also much cheaper than 50 gm balls).

Because knitting is so stretchy, it needs sewing up with a stitch that stretches, like back stitch. Work in small neat stitches near the edge. Very bulky stitch patterns need to be oversewn, or the seams will be too thick, but again sew as small and as neatly as possible.

One of the neatest seams is grafting, that is putting the two edges together side by side with the right sides towards you, and, with needle and thread, grafting the two edges together by taking a stitch from each piece in turn, row by row. This means of course that the pieces must match completely row for row. Grafting is ideal for fine and small garments where a bulky seam would look out of place.

chosen stitch pattern is one which rolls up anyway.

When inserting sleeves, seam sides up to carefully measured armholes, match the sleeve seam to the garment side seam, then the top centre of the sleeve to the shoulder seam. Ease any fullness evenly between, especially with a dropped sleeve. A set-in sleeve can have fullness eased towards the top to accommodate the shoulder.

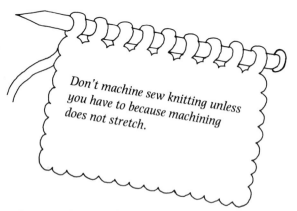

Don't machine sew knitting unless you have to because machining does not stretch.

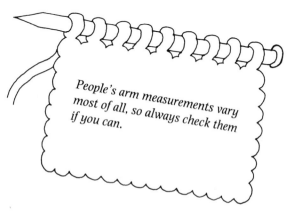

People's arm measurements vary most of all, so always check them if you can.

SIMPLE SLEEVES

Sleeves can be completely straight. This means they fit into a dropped shoulder and are very full at the wrist. If they have a welt at the wrist, then the number of stitches for this welt needs to be much decreased if it is to fit. Such sleeves are simply set into an armhole created in the side seam of the garment. If you design these sleeves yourself, think in terms of a normal armhole being about 8 ins deep so that at the top, the sleeve must be 16 ins wide, and the cuff welt needs the number of stitches equivalent to about 10 ins in all. So, with straight sleeves, you need a row next to the welt which alters the number of stitches appropriately. (See the sleeves of Snow White on page 91.) Or, such straight sleeves need not have welts at all, but can have hems (as in Bright on page 124) or could simply roll back into a cuff, especially if the

SURFACE DECORATION

One of the easiest ways to decorate knitting, without using elaborate stitch patterns, is to stitch things on to it. Embroidery is useful too, but that comes later (see page 116), but, more simply, any three-dimensional goodies can be stitched on. Beads, buttons, ribbons, fur, fabric, feathers and anything decorative that isn't too heavy can turn a plain garment into something spectacular and original. This technique can be used with existing or even bought garments and is very easy to do, or even to alter. Why not have a basic white or neutral jumper and change the sewn-on decoration to match different outfits or your mood? Make a bias strip from matching fabric and bind a jumper with it, or stitch on fabric pockets, cuffs, collars or patch patterns. Cover buttons with fabric to fasten a knitted cardigan, or decorate a jumper.

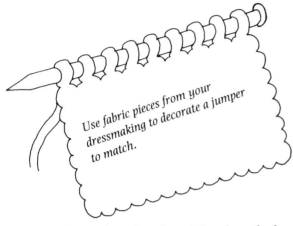

Use fabric pieces from your dressmaking to decorate a jumper to match.

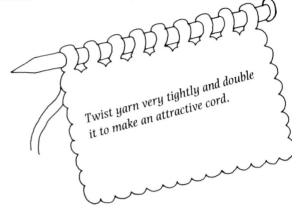

Twist yarn very tightly and double it to make an attractive cord.

Two more formal and traditional methods of adding decoration are the threading of eyelet holes with ribbon, and bead knitting. Eyelet holes are added simply by working two stitches together and then making a stitch by putting the yarn round the needle. When knitted back on the next row, this makes a hole, and lots of these arranged in a row can be threaded. This is, of course, the very simple principle behind lace knitting (see page 111). Such threaded necks need to be a good fit, otherwise they gather the garment like a sack of spuds. This is the reason for the variations in the pattern for Snow White on page 90.

Threaded eyelets have always been used to fasten garments, particularly baby things, but please, if you use them for this, firmly stitch the ribbon in, as unthreaded ribbon is potentially dangerous for tiny babies. But threaded eyelets make lovely decoration on waist or wrist fastenings and, as well as ribbon, you can thread with twisted cords, plaits, leather, bought braid and cords, bias strip, tinsel . . . anything!

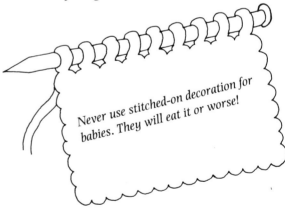

Never use stitched-on decoration for babies. They will eat it or worse!

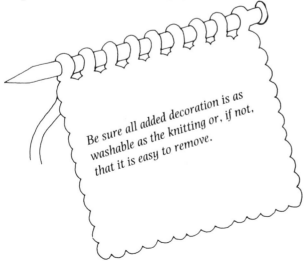

Be sure all added decoration is as washable as the knitting or, if not, that it is easy to remove.

BEAD KNITTING

This patient technique is a way of knitting in the beads, rather than sewing them on afterwards, and can be very beautiful. Choose a fine yarn and beads that have a large enough hole for the yarn to pass through freely. Thread the beads on the yarn, and use the yarn through the beads as you knit, bringing a bead up to the work when you want it and knit it into the stitch. There are several ways of making this process easier.

Plan carefully. If the garment takes 10 balls of yarn, and 100 beads evenly spaced, it is no good threading all 100 beads on to the first ball, as 90 of them will shoot all over the floor when the first ball runs out!

Threading beads on yarn can be tricky, so to make it easier take a fine beading needle threaded double with sewing cotton to make a loop. Through this loop put a long end of yarn and thread the beads on to the cotton first, then the yarn.

If the beads are in a colour pattern, arrange them first then thread them on to the yarn *backwards*, because, of course, the first bead you will use, will be the last bead you threaded.

Beads knit most easily into raised stitches. That is right side, purl stitches, so if you can, arrange your stitch pattern to coincide with this.

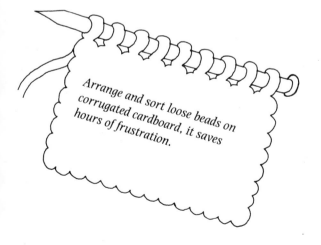

Arrange and sort loose beads on corrugated cardboard, it saves hours of frustration.

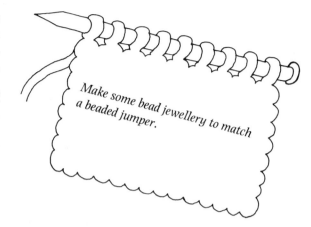

Make some bead jewellery to match a beaded jumper.

'SNOW WHITE'

This jumper has very simple straight dropped sleeves, worked from the top down because this is easier, involving just a decreasing row before the cuff welt. It is decorated with tiny, pearlised bead buttons sewn on later, although you could, of course, knit beads in or decorate it with anything you liked. The garment in the photograph has a simple round neck like Matelot, but the pattern also gives the alternative shown in the drawing: a ribbon threaded frilled neck. Frills are easy. Just increase a lot in one row to give many more stitches.

Materials

Wendy Dolce in Cream. 8(8,9,9,10) × 50 gm balls. For decoration: approximately 100 pearl buttons from Glamor. No. JHB 22758, and ribbon for the optional, frilled-necked version. 1 pr. 4 mm (No. 8) needles. 1 pr. 3¼ mm (No. 10) needles. (Or alter to suit your tension if required.)

Tension

24 sts and 32 rows = 4 ins (10 cms) in st.st. on 4 mm (No. 8) needles.

Sizes

To fit 32(34,36,38,40) ins with 3 ins of ease.

Back

Using needles two sizes smaller than those chosen for main tension, e.g. 3¼ mm (No. 10) needles, cast on 105(111,117,123,129) sts and work 2½ ins in K1,P1 rib, beginning and ending every row K, and keeping rib correct in between.*

Change to needles chosen for main tension e.g. 4 mm (No. 8), and st.st., and work straight to a total measurement of 23 ins ending with a P row.

Plain neck version:
Next row Cast off 28(31,34,37,39) sts, K until 28(31,34,37,39) sts rem. Place the 49(49, 49,49,51) sts just worked on to a holder. Cast off to end.

Frilled neck version:
Next row Cast off 32(35,38,41,43) sts, K until 32(35,38,41,43) sts rem. Place the 41(41, 41,41,43) sts just worked on to a holder. Cast off to end.

Front

Work as given for Back as far as *, change to larger needles and st.st., and work straight to a total measurement of 19 ins, ending with a P row.

Plain neck version:
Shape neck K40(43,46,49,52) sts, turn, and work this side first.
**Dec. 1 st. at neck edge on next 6(6,6,6,7) rows, then every alt. row 6 times. (28,31,34,37,39 sts rem.)
Work straight until Front matches Back at armhole edge, ending with a P row.
Cast off**.
Place centre 25(25,25,25,25) sts on a holder, rejoin yarn to rem. sts, K to end.
Rep. from ** to **.

Frilled neck version:
Shape neck K44(47,50,53,56) sts, turn, and work this side first.
††Dec. 1 st. at neck edge on next 6(6,6,6,7) rows, then every alt. row 6 times. (32,35,38,41,43 sts rem.)
Work straight until Front matches Back at armhole edge, ending with a P row.
Cast off††.
Place centre 17 sts on to a holder, rejoin yarn to rem. sts K to end.
Rep. from †† to ††.

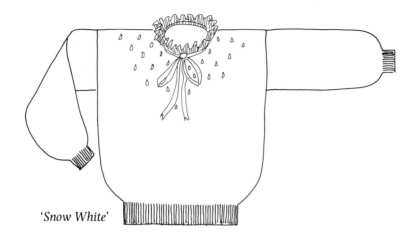

'Snow White'

Sleeves (Worked 'upside down', because it's easier!)

With *larger* needles, cast on 94(98,106,114,118) sts and work straight in st.st. to a total measurement of 16 ins, ending with a P row.
Next row (K2tog.) to end. (47,49,53,57,59 sts)
Change to smaller needles and work 2½ ins in K1,P1 rib in the same way as given for the Back. Cast off very loosely in rib.

Neckband (Both versions)

Using back stitch, carefully join left shoulder seam. Using smaller needles, with right side facing, pick up and K the stitches from the back neck holder (working 2 together in the middle), 29(29, 29,33,35) sts down the left front slope, the stitches from the front neck holder, and 29(29,29,33,35) sts up the right front slope.

Plain neck version:
Work 12 rows in K1,P1 rib. Cast off in rib.

Frilled neck version:
Work 5 rows in K1,P1 rib in the same way as given for the Back.
Next row (Making ribbon eyelet holes) K1(1,1,1,4),

(yon., K2tog., K2tog.tbl., yon., K5) to last 6(6,6,5,8) sts, yon., K2tog., K2tog.tbl., yon., K2(2,2,1,4).
Next row K.
Next row In K, inc. 1 st in every st.
K5 rows. Cast off.

Making Up

Do not press or brush. Join all rem. seams to give an armhole depth of 8(8,9,9½,10) ins. Add the decorations.

BRUSHING

Some yarns are already brushed. That is they are fluffy like the yarn in which the previous jumper was knitted, but, if you wish, you can brush them still more when your knitting is completed. This used to be, and still can be, done with teazles, or you can buy a small brush from your wool shop. You can be surprisingly tough with these and make some yarns, especially mohairs, very fluffy indeed. The 'wrong' side of stocking stitch, called reversed stocking stitch (rev.st.st.), will also brush up very well.

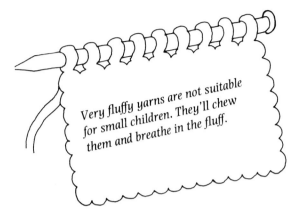

Very fluffy yarns are not suitable for small children. They'll chew them and breathe in the fluff.

INCREASING

There are several ways of increasing. One or more stitches can be cast on at the beginning of a row, or, after knitting into the front of a stitch in the usual way, do not remove the old stitch from the needle but knit into the back of it as well, before going on to the next stitch.

An invisible method is to pick up the loop of yarn between two stitches and knit into the back of it, so creating a new stitch in between. (6, 7 and 8)

Another form of virtually invisible increasing is to pick up and knit into the stitch below the next stitch, and then knit the next stitch in the usual way.

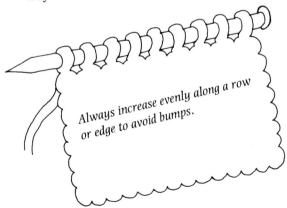

Always increase evenly along a row or edge to avoid bumps.

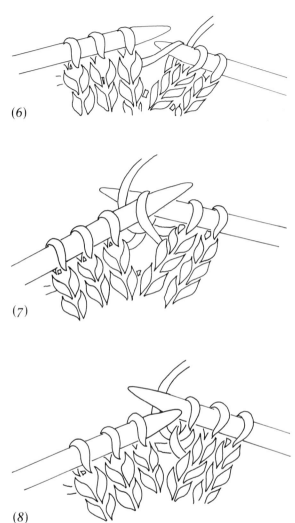

(6)

(7)

(8)

SLIPPED OR LOOP STITCH PATTERNS

Lacey patterns can be easily created, without actually knitting lace, by making long stitches. These are made by simply winding the yarn more than once around the working needle when knitting, then, on the following row dropping the extra loops off the needle. You can add as many loops as you wish, the more loops the lacier the result, and the effect is similar to that achieved by working on enormous needles. Or you could try working on one enormous and one much smaller needle, used alternately. The result of all these techniques is, as well as providing the laceyness, to make the work grow with satisfying speed.

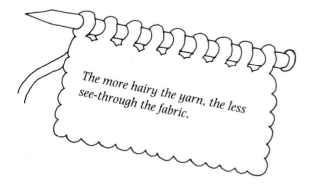

The more hairy the yarn, the less see-through the fabric.

'SOFTY'

Still keeping to our simple style, this garment introduces mohair, a luxury fashion yarn from Angora goats. (Yes goats, not rabbits, confusing isn't it?) The stitch pattern is based on slip-loop stitches of varying length, which create a waved effect, which has to be alternated on the following row to keep the fabric square.

This is the first garment in the series to use increasing, as the sleeves are shaped by increasing from wrist to shoulder in the conventional way. Because of the slipped stitches, the rows are far apart, so the increasing comes more often than would be expected with ordinary stocking stitch.

Materials

Patons Mohair Focus. Green. 12(13,15) × 25 gm balls. 1 pr. 5½ mm (No. 5) needles. 1 pr 4½ mm (No. 7) needles. (Or alter to suit your tension.)

Tension

15 sts and 20 rows = 4 ins (10 cms) on 5½ mm (No. 5) needles in st.st.

Sizes

To fit 32–34(36–38,40–42) ins.
Actual size 36(41,46) ins.

Special Abbreviation

K1yo2, K1yo3, etc. = Knit one, putting the yarn around the needle twice, three times, etc. instead of the usual once. On the following row the stitch is worked through one of these loops only, the remainder of the loops being dropped off to form elongated stitches.
N.B. Take care not to leave a loop on the needle if it should be dropped. This gives a gradually increasing number of stitches!

Stitch Pattern

Rows 1 & 2 K.
Row 3 K6, *K1yo2, K1yo3, K1yo4, K1yo3, K1yo2, K5*, rep. from * to * to last st., K1.
Row 4 K, dropping all extra loops.
Rows 5 & 6 K.
Row 7 K1, K1yo2, K1yo3, K1yo4, K1yo3, K1yo2, *K5, K1yo2, K1yo3, K1yo4, K1yo3, K1yo2*, rep. from * to * to last st., K1.
Row 8 As row 4.
Rep. these 8 rows throughout as required.

Back

Using needles two sizes smaller than those chosen for main tension e.g. 4½ mm (No. 7), cast on 67(77,87) sts and work 3 ins in K1,P1 rib beginning and ending every row K, and keeping rib correct in between.*

Change to stitch pattern and needles chosen for main tension, e.g. 5½ mm (No. 5), and work straight to a total measurement of approx. 23 ins ending with either Row 2 or Row 6 of the pattern.
Next row Cast off 18(23,27), K until 18(23,27) sts rem., place 31(31,33) sts just worked on to a holder. Cast off rem. sts.

Front

Work as for Back as far as *.
Change to stitch pattern and larger needles and work straight to a total measurement of approx. 19 ins, ending with either Row 2 or Row 6 of the pattern.
Shape neck Keeping pattern correct, and noting that the yarn should not be wound round the needle more than once at sts at row ends, i.e. begin and end every row with plain K1.
Next row Pattern 26(31,36) turn, and complete this side first.
**Keeping pattern correct, dec. 1 st at neck edge on next five rows, then on every alt. row 3(3,4) times. (18,23,27 sts rem.)
Work straight until armhole edge matches that on the Back, ending with row 2 or row 6.
Cast off**.
Place centre 15 sts on to a holder.
Rejoin yarn to rem. sts and rep. from ** to **.

Sleeves

Using smaller needles, cast on 37(37,37) sts and work 2½ ins in K1,P1 rib in the same way as given for the Back. Change to larger needles and stitch pattern and, keeping stitch pattern correct, increase 1 st. each end of every 4th (4th,3rd) row, keeping end sts of every row in K as on the neck shaping, until there are 63(67,71) sts.
Work straight to a total measurement of 18(18,17) ins ending with row 2 or row 6 of the pattern.
Cast off loosely.

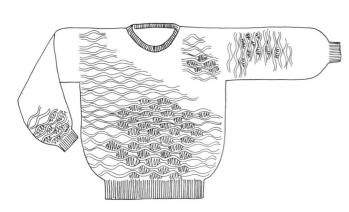

'Softy'

Neckband

Using back stitch carefully join left shoulder seam. Using smaller needles, with right side facing, pick up and K the 31(31,33) sts from the back neck holder, working 2tog. in the middle, 19(19,21) sts down the left front neck slope, the 15 sts from the front neck holder, and 19(19,21) sts up the right front neck. (83,83,89 sts.)

Work 8 rows in K1,P1 rib in the same way as for the Back.

Cast off loosely in rib.

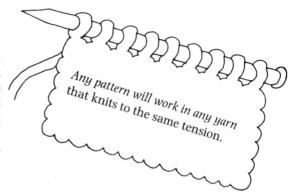

Any pattern will work in any yarn that knits to the same tension.

Making Up

Do not press or brush. Carefully join rem. seams, matching all pattern and shapings, using back stitch, and leaving armholes 8½(9,9½) ins deep.

ADAPTING AND ALTERING PATTERNS

If you prefer to knit from a commercial pattern, but can't find exactly what you want, here are a few ideas on adapting an existing design.

To add a V neck to a round-neck pattern, like our simple pattern, decide how deep you would like the V to be and mark a centre stitch at this depth. The remaining neck stitches then need to be lost, half at each side, evenly up each slope. Measure your neck depth, count the number of rows per inch you have at your tension, and so work out the total number of rows in the whole neck. Share the decreasing evenly between these rows. It is always worth measuring underarm and body length on the person who will wear the jumper and altering this on the pattern to suit them.

How much yarn do you need for a pattern you have altered or designed yourself? The best way to assess this is to make a guesstimate based on a similar commercial pattern in your chosen yarn. Wool shops will usually take excess yarn back if you don't keep it too long. So it is best to over

estimate a little. Or weigh a similar finished garment.

Patterns of similar tensions can be mixed and matched. The sleeves of one into the armholes of the other, and so on. But do not mix shapes that won't go. To take an exaggerated example, a raglan sleeve won't fit a set-in armhole, but a shirt collar can be worked instead of a polo neck, or cuffs added to straight sleeves.

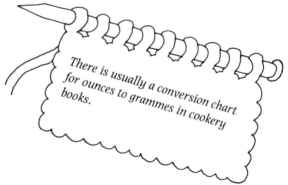

There is usually a conversion chart for ounces to grammes in cookery books.

ARMHOLE SHAPES

So far, all of these jumpers have had the simplest dropped armhole, created by working straight to shoulder height. Traditionally this is altered in two main ways, to create a set-in sleeve, or a raglan.

Raglan shaping simply loses all the stitches gradually and evenly on all the garment pieces

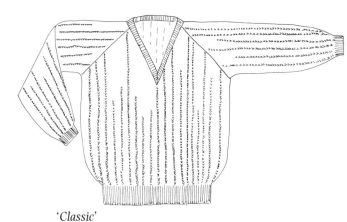

'Classic'

between armhole and neckband. It is often decreased decoratively a few stitches in on plain jumpers to add interesting detail. (See alternative Classic, page 98).

Set-in sleeves are the classic, tailored shape with some stitches taken out at the bottom of the armhole, some removed gradually and the rest worked straight to the shoulder, with the sleeve shaped to match.

HOW STITCH PATTERNS AFFECT TENSION

As we saw in the previous jumper, where the rows were widely spread by the dropped loops on the stitches, a stitch pattern can easily affect the tension and, if a garment is in an all-over stitch pattern, it may be necessary to do a tension square in the stitch pattern. Rib patterns in particular eat up stitch numbers.

'CLASSIC'

This men's jumper is in the classic V-necked, set-in sleeve style, worked in a slipped-stitch mock-rib pattern. An alternative is given for the raglan style shown in the drawing.

Materials

Patons Siberia Russet: 10(11,11,12,12,13) × 50 gm balls.
1 pr. 5½ mm (No. 5) needles. 1 pr. 4½ mm (No. 7) needles. (Or alter to suit your tension, if required.)

Tension

15 sts and 20 rows = 4 ins (10 cms) on 5½ mm (No. 5) needles in st.st. Over stitch pattern on the same needles: 18 sts = 4 ins (10 cms).

Sizes

To fit 34(36,38,40,42,44) ins.

Back

Using needles two sizes smaller than those chosen for main tension, e.g. 4½ mm (No. 7), cast on 67(71,75,79,83,87) sts and work 2½ ins in K1,P1 rib, beginning and ending every row K and keeping rib correct in between.

Next row (Keeping rib correct) rib3, *inc. 1 st. in next st., rib3*, rep. from * to * to end. (83,88,93, 98,103,108 sts.)

Change to needles chosen for main tension, e.g. 5½ mm (No. 5), and slip st. mock rib pattern:

Row 1 K3,*sl.2 purlwise, K3*, rep. from * to * to end.

Row 2 P.

Rep. these 2 rows throughout.

Work straight in pattern until work measures 15(15,15½,15½,15½,15½) ins, ending with a P row.

Shape armholes (set-in sleeve version):

Keeping pattern correct throughout, cast off 4(4,5,5,6,6) sts at beg. of next 2 rows.**

Continuing to keep pattern correct, dec. 1 st. each end of next 3 rows, then every alt. row until 57(60,63,66,69,72) sts rem.

Work straight in pattern until armholes measure 8(8,8½,9,9,9½) ins ending with a P row.

Shape shoulders

Continuing to keep pattern correct, cast off 6(6,6,7,7,7) sts at the beg. of the next 4 rows, then 5(6.7.6.7.8) sts at the beg. of the next 2 rows.

Place rem. 23(24,25,26,27,28) sts on to a holder.

Front

Work as given for back as far as **.

Shape armholes and neck Continuing to keep pattern correct.

Next row K2tog., pattern 35(37,39,41,43,45) sts, turn, and work this side first:

***Continuing to keep pattern correct, dec. 1 st. at armhole edge on next 2 rows, then every alt. row 6(7,7,8,8,9) times, at the same time, dec. 1 st. at neck edge on next and every foll. 3rd row until 17(18,19,20,21,22) sts rem.

Work straight until armhole measures same as on the Back, ending at the armhole edge.

Cast off 6(6,6,7,7,7) sts at beg. of next and foll. alt. row.

Work 1 row.

Cast off rem. 5(6,7,6,7,8) sts.***

Rejoin yarn to rem. sts at inside edge.

1st, 3rd, and 5th sizes only, K1.

2nd, 4th, and 6th sizes only, K2tog.

Place this st. on a pin, pattern to end.

Next row P2tog.tbl., P to end.

Rep. as for other side from *** to ***.

Sleeves (Set-in Version)

Using smaller needles, cast on 38(38,38,43,43,43) sts and work 2½ ins in K1,P1 rib in the same way as for the Back.

Change to larger needles and pattern as before, and inc. 1 st. each end of every 6th(6th,5th,5th,5th,4th) row until there are 56(60,64,67,71,75) sts, working all increases into the pattern.

Work straight to a total measurement of 18(18,18½,18½,19,19) ins or desired measurement to under-arm, ending with a P row.

Continuing to keep pattern correct, cast off 4(4,5,5,6,6) sts at beg of next 2 rows.†

Dec. 1 st. at each end of the next 2 rows, then every alt. row until 20(22,22,23,23,23) sts rem.

Dec. 1 st. each end of the next 3 rows, then cast off 4 sts at the beg. of the foll. 2 rows.

Cast off rem. 6(8,8,9,9,9) sts.

Neckband

Do not press. Using back stitch, and matching all shapings and pattern, carefully join the left shoulder seam.

With right side facing, pick up and K the

23(24,25,26,27,28) sts from the back neck holder, 37(36,39,40,41,42) sts evenly down the left neck slope, the st. from the pin, leaving the pin to mark the st., and 36(36,38,40,42,42) sts evenly up the right neck slope. (97,97,103,107,111,113 sts)

††*Next row* K1(P1,K1) to 3 sts before the marked st., P1,K2tog., P1, K2tog., (P1,K1) to end.

Next row Rib to 2 sts before the marked st., P2tog., K1, P2tog., rib to end.

Next row Rib to 2 sts before the marked st, K2tog., P1,K2tog., rib to end.

Rep. the last 2 rows until 9 rows of rib have been worked in all.

Cast off loosely in rib, decreasing in the same way on this row also.

Making Up

Do not press. Join all rem. seams carefully in back st. matching all pattern and shapings.

Raglan Alternative to 'CLASSIC':

Work the Back in the same way as given as far as ** then shape raglan keeping pattern correct:

Next row K1, K2tog.tbl., pattern to last 3 sts, K2tog., K1.

Next row K1, P to last st., K1.

Rep. these 2 rows until there are 47 (56,53,58,63,68) sts ending with the P row.

Next row K1, K2tog.tbl., pattern to last 3 sts, K2tog., K1.

Next row K1, P2tog., P to last 3 sts, P2tog.tbl., K1.
Rep. these 2 rows until 23(24,25,26,27,28) sts rem. Leave these sts on a holder.

Work front in the same way as for the back as far as **, then shape raglan and neck, keeping pattern correct:

Next row K1, K2tog.tbl., pattern 34 (36,38,40,42,44) sts, turn, and work this side first:
†††Continuing to keep pattern correct, dec. 1 st at neck edge on every 3rd row 11(11,12,12,13,13)

times, at the same time, dec. at raglan edge in the same way as for the Back on every alt. row 14(12,15,15,14,14) times, then on every row until 2 sts rem. keeping neck edge straight when dec. on this edge is complete.

Work 2tog., fasten off.†††
Rejoin yarn to rem. sts at inside edge.

1st, 3rd and 5th sizes only, K1.
2nd, 4th and 6th sizes only, K2 tog.
Place this st. on a pin, pattern to last 3 sts, K2tog., K1.

Rep. as for other side from ††† to †††.

Work sleeves as given as far as †, then shape raglan on every alt. row in the same way as for the Back until 12(18,18,17,21,25) sts rem., then on every row until 4(6,6,5,5,5) sts rem.
Leave these sts on a holder.

Neckband

Do not press. Using back stitch carefully join both front and left back raglan seams. With right side facing pick up and K the 23(24,25,26,27,28) sts from the back neck holder, 4(6,6,5,5,5) sts from the left sleeve, 37(36,39,41,44,43) sts evenly down the left neck slope, the st. from the pin, (leaving the pin in to mark the st.), 36(36,38,41,43,43) sts evenly up the right front slope, and 4(6,6,5,5,5) sts from the right sleeve. (105,109,115,119, 125,125 sts.)
Work as given for main pattern from ††.

ARAN STITCH PATTERNS

One of the reasons for complex stitch patterns like those found in Aran patterns is, of course, that they add depth and therefore insulation, making the garment warmer. Cold areas, or professions, originate garments with elaborate patterns. Fishing off the Isles of Aran can be a pretty cold business, and the knitters of Aran made a virtue of necessity and made this practical insulation decorative too, as well as full of Folklore and legend.

Many of these three-dimensional patterns involve twisting and reversing groups of stitches, typically cables, in which a small number of stitches are held to the back or front of the work, the next few stitches are worked, and then the ones from the cable needle are knitted. You will only need a few sizes of cable needle as the stitches are only held on them and not knitted with them.

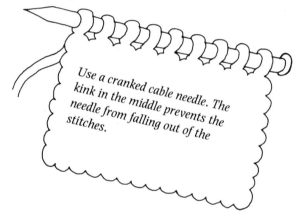

Use a cranked cable needle. The kink in the middle prevents the needle from falling out of the stitches.

Cables can become very elaborate, like all other Celtic plaited patterns, and with the other textured Aran stitches like bobbles and all-over patterns, they have possibilities for endless variation, beauty and as much complexity as you wish. Before you tackle the cable pattern, study the Aran abbreviations on page 100, and perhaps practise a few on bits of knitting.

Many of the traditional patterns have now been written down and collected like folk songs, and they are often written as a single stitch pattern that creates a vertical panel of texture. (See Bibliography on page 139.) These can be put together in any way you wish, traditionally symmetrically around a central panel, although you can work them irregularly, horizontally, diagonally or all four ways if you wish!

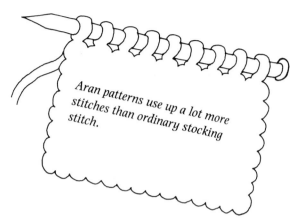

Aran patterns use up a lot more stitches than ordinary stocking stitch.

If you work out your own pattern, do remember to allow for the number of stitches that thick Aran textures use up. If you choose a favourite stocking stitch jumper pattern and work it in panels of Aran, it will come out far too small. So do knit a large tension sample, and add extra panels if necessary.

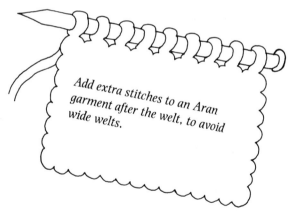

Add extra stitches to an Aran garment after the welt, to avoid wide welts.

'COTTON CABLES'

The Aran slipover patterned here has an increasing row at the end of the welt to add the number of stitches needed for the Aran pattern. For the pattern as photographed, I chose the stitch patterns I liked, and the drawing shows another pos-

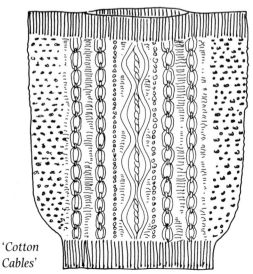

'Cotton Cables'

sible variation with other patterns. Because the yarn is a soft cotton, the welts are knitted on needles three sizes smaller instead of two, and knitting elastic, together with the yarn, is used to make the welts firm and lasting. The neck rib needs no elastic, it would tighten it too much. Be sure to make the neck opening generous enough.

Materials

Wendy Fiori Cotton in Orange: 11(12,14) × 50 gm balls. 1 small reel of knitting elastic. 1 pr. 5½ mm (No. 5) needles. 1 pr. 4 mm (No. 8) needles. (Or alter to suit your tension if required.)

Tension

16 sts and 22 rows = 4 ins (10 cms) on 5½ mm (No. 5) needles in st.st.

Sizes

To fit up to 36(up to 40, up to 44) ins.
Actual measurements 39(42,45) ins.

Aran Abbreviations

cr5 = cross 5, i.e. place next 2 sts on a cable needle, and leave at front of work, K2,P1, then K2 from cable needle.

cr3r = cross 3 right, i.e. place next st on cable needle, and leave at back of work, K2, then P1 from cable needle.

cr3l = cross 3 left, i.e. place next 2 sts on a cable needle and leave at front of work, P1, then K2 from cable needle.

c4b = cable 4 back, i.e. place next 2 sts on a cable needle and leave at back of work, K2, then K2 from cable needle.

c4f = cable 4 front, i.e. place next 2 sts on a cable needle and leave at front of work, K2, then K2 from cable needle.

mb=make bobble, i.e. K into the front, then the back, then the front, then the back of the next st., only removing it from the needle after this 4th st., turn and P4, turn and K4, turn and P4, turn and K4tog.

Trinity Stitch

Row 1 (Right side) P.
Row 2 K1,* work (K1,P1,K1) all in next st., P3tog.*
Rep. from * to * to last st., K1.
Row 3 P.
Row 4 K1* P3tog., work (K1,P1,K1) all in next st.*
Rep. from * to * to last st., K1.
Rep. these 4 rows throughout Trinity Stitch sections.

Back and Front (Both alike)

Using needles three sizes smaller than those chosen for main tension, e.g. 4 mm (No. 8), and yarn and elastic knitted together, cast on 77(83,89) sts and work 2½ ins in K1,P1 rib, and working first and last st. in every row K, and keeping rib correct in between.
Next row Rib 12(13,14)*. Inc. 1 st. in next st., rib 1*, rep. from * to * to last 11(12,13), rib to end. (104,112,120 sts)
Break off elastic and weave in the end, and change to needles chosen for main tension, e.g. 5½ mm (No. 5), and work in pattern:
Row 1 P6(10,14), **K4, P1, K4, P6, cr5, P6, K4, P1, K4**, P22, rep. from ** to **, P6(10,14).
Row 2 K1, rep. from * to * of Row 2 of Trinity Stitch 1 (2,3) times, K1,**, P4, K1, P4, K6, P2, K1, P2, K6, P4, K1, P4**, K1. Rep. from * to * of Row 2 of Trinity Stitch 5 times, K1, rep. from ** to **, K1, rep. from * to * of Row 2 of Trinity Stitch 1 (2, 3) times, K1.
Row 3 P6(10,14), **K4, P1, K4, P5, cr3r, K1, cr3l, P5, K4, P1, K4**, P22, rep. from ** to **, P6(10,14).

Row 4 K1, rep. from * to * of Row 4 of Trinity Stitch 1 (2,3) times, K1, **P4, K1, P4, K5, P2, K1, P1, K1, P2, K5, P4, K1, P4**, K1, rep. from * to * of Row 4 of Trinity Stitch 5 times, K1, rep. from ** to **, K1, rep. from * to * of Row 4 of Trinity Stitch 1 (2, 3) times, K1.
These 4 rows form Trinity Stitch for first and last 6(10,14) sts, and centre 22 sts and will now be referred to as 'Patt' (i.e. pattern) throughout.
Row 5 Patt 6(10,14), **c4f, mb, c4b, P4, cr3r, K1, P1, K1, cr3l, P4, c4b, mb, c4f**, Patt 22, rep. from ** to **, Patt 6(10,14).
Row 6 Patt 6(10,14), **P4, K1, P4, K4, P2, K1, (P1, K1) twice, P2, K4, P4, K1, P4**, Patt 22, rep. from ** to **, Patt 6(10,14).
Row 7 Patt 6(10,14), **K4, P1, K4, P3, cr3r, K1, (P1,K1) twice, cr3l, P3, K4, P1, K4**, Patt 22, rep. from ** to **, Patt 6(10,14).
Row 8 Patt 6(10,14), **P4, K1, P4, K3, P2, K1, (P1,K1) 3 times, P2, K3, P4, K1, P4**, Patt 22, rep. from ** to **, Patt 6(10,14).
Row 9 Patt 6(10,14), **K4, P1, K4, P2, cr3r, K1, (P1,K1) 3 times, cr3l, P2, K4, P1, K4**, Patt 22, rep. from ** to **, Patt 6(10,14).
Row 10 Patt 6(10,14), **P4, K1, P4, K2, P2, K1, (P1,K1) 4 times, P2, K2, P4, K1, P4**, Patt 22, rep. from ** to **, Patt 6(10,14).
Row 11 Patt 6(10,14), **c4f, mb, c4b, P2, cr3l, P1, (K1,P1) 3 times, cr3r, P2, c4b, mb, c4f**, Patt 22, rep. from ** to **, Patt 6(10,14).
Row 12 As Row 8.
Row 13 Patt 6(10,14), **K4, P1, K4, P3, cr3l, P1, (K1,P1) twice, cr3r, P3, K4, P1, K4**, Patt 22, rep. from ** to **, Patt 6(10,14).
Row 14 As Row 6.
Row 15 Patt 6(10,14), **K4, P1, K4, P4, cr3l, P1, K1, P1, cr3r, P4, K4, P1, K4**, Patt 22, rep. from ** to **, Patt 6(10,14).
Row 16 As Row 4.
Row 17 Patt 6(10,14), **c4f, mb, c4b, P5, cr3l, P1, cr3r, P5, c4b, mb, c4f**, Patt 22, rep. from ** to **, Patt 6(10,14).

Row 18 As Row 2.

Rep. these 18 rows, keeping 4 row Trinity Stitch pattern correct until work measures approximately 22 ins, ending with the next 18th row.

Without changing needles and without adding elastic, work 2 ins in K1, P1 rib in the same way as for the welt, working 2tog. at the beg. of the first row. Cast off in rib.

Making Up and Armbands

Do not press. Carefully and as invisibly as possible, oversew the two shoulder seams leaving an 11(11,12) inch neck opening.

At each armhole edge, mark a point on the back and front 9(9,9½) ins down from the shoulder seam.

With right side facing, using smaller needles, pick up and K 36(36,38) sts up to the shoulder seam evenly, at the rate of 4 sts per inch, then 37(37,39) sts down to the 2nd marked point. (73,73,77 sts.)

Work 8 rows in K1,P1 rib in the same way as for the welt, but without elastic.

Carefully make up side seams in backstitch.

ARAN AS DECORATION

The Aran patterns, like cables and bobbles, also make lovely decoration on their own for other patterns. As you get more expert, try working them in a contrast colour. Looks terrific.

Work knitting elastic together with any non-stretch yarn in the welts.

KNITTING ELASTIC

This is an excellent method of adding stretch to welts on non-stretch yarns, but also on welts that take a lot of wear, such as children's jumpers, or for any garment that looks better with a tight welt. It looks like fine fishing line, but is quite strong and is available from wool shops.

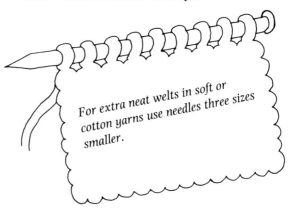

For extra neat welts in soft or cotton yarns use needles three sizes smaller.

COLOUR KNITTING

If you are frightened of picture knitting, don't be! It is much easier than it looks, especially if you start with something simple and something that is not meant to be anything, like the splodgy jumper 'Double Cream' on page 104. If you try to knit a perfect Siamese cat picture and it goes all wrong, everyone will notice. With a splodgy jumper, no one even knows. Try the technique on a small piece first, perhaps the tension square or a blanket square; so, if you really dislike doing it, you won't quit half way through an expensive mistake.

Join in a new colour a few stitches before it is needed in the same way as you would weave in yarn for Fair Isle (see page 122) then, every time you change colour, twist the new round the old, leave the old colour behind and continue with the new. This really does work, and makes a strong neat fabric. (*9 and 10*)

Try new techniques on a small sample rather than on a whole garment.

Cut shorter lengths of yarn for colour knitting, it doesn't take a 50 gm ball to knit Postman Pat's hat!

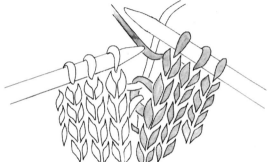

(9) *Twisting two colours on a knit row*

Estimate how much each patch of colour will take and cut it off the ball. If it is too short you can always weave in some more. Short pieces are easily untangled, longer pieces can be wound on to bits of card, or specially bought plastic yarn bobbins, to dangle out of harm's way at the back of the work. All this avoids glorious birds-nests of yarn, and a cat's paradise of 50 gm balls rolling around the furniture legs. If you are doing large patches of colour, put whole balls of yarn in a holder of some kind to prevent this kind of fuddle. Big jam jars are ideal.

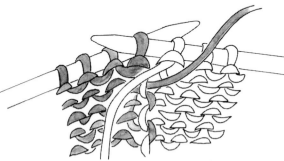

(10) *Twisting two colours on a purl row*

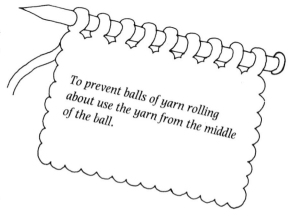

To prevent balls of yarn rolling about use the yarn from the middle of the ball.

Every time that you begin a new colour across a row, start a separate length of yarn. This sounds difficult, but is much easier and very much neater than stranding colours across the back.

Colour knitting should not affect tension, but, if you find that yours does, remember to allow for it and use different needles.

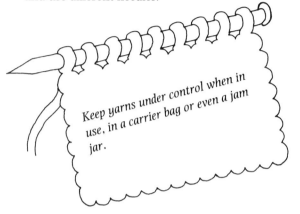

Keep yarns under control when in use, in a carrier bag or even a jam jar.

Double up thin yarns to make them knit to a similar tension as thicker yarns.

'DOUBLE CREAM'

This is our familiar simple pattern, but worked in patches of different yarns. These yarns are different textures of similar colours, but yours could be the same yarn in different colours, or a wild mixture of both.

One of the yarns looked good in reversed stocking stitch, so the areas of this are simply worked the other way round. That is, knitted when the other yarns would have been purled, and vice versa.

An average tension was chosen at which all the yarns looked good. To achieve it, one of the yarns, which was much thinner than the others, was used double. If in doubt about this, use yarns that all work to the same recommended tension.

The textured areas on this jumper were done at random and for fun, in any way that I thought looked good. Follow the pattern drawing if you want your jumper just the same, done in inches, not stitches, as there is no need to be accurate with this kind of colour knitting, but you can, of course, do your patches in any way you wish.

The other addition to this pattern is a square neck. The simplest of all to pattern for yourself. Just leave the number of stitches needed for the neck on a holder in the middle and work the two sides separately, straight to the shoulder. The neck rib is then worked like a double V neck, with a point at each front corner.

'DOUBLE CREAM'

Materials

Wendy Capri White: 3(3,3,3,3,4,4) × 50 gm balls.
Wendy Como White: 2(2,2,2,2,2,2) × 50 gm balls.
Wendy Pampas White: 2(2,2,2,2,2,2) × 50 gm balls.
Wendy Dolce White: 1(1,1,1,2,2,2) × 50 gm balls.
1 small reel of knitting elastic.
1 pr. 5 mm (No. 6) needles. 1 pr. 4 mm (No. 8) needles. (Or alter to suit your tension if required.)

Tension

In all the yarns, (but using Pampas *only*, *double*), 20 sts and 29 rows = 4 ins (10 cms) on 5 mm (No. 6) needles in st.st.
N.B. The row tension is not as important and will alter from yarn to yarn a little. To achieve a stitch tension, I suggest you do a little strip with a stripe of each and get as near as you can to an average of 20 sts.

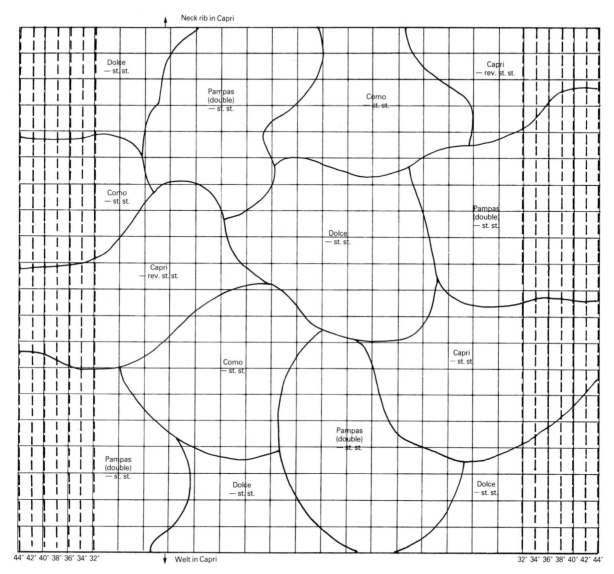

Neck rib in Capri

Dolce
— st. st.

Pampas
(double)
— st. st.

Como
— st. st.

Capri
— rev. st. st.

Como
— st. st.

Dolce
— st. st.

Pampas
(double)
— st. st.

Capri
— rev. st. st.

Como
— st. st.

Capri
— st. st.

Pampas
(double)
— st. st.

Pampas
(double)
— st. st.

Dolce
— st. st.

Dolce
— st. st.

44″ 42″ 40″ 38″ 36″ 34″ 32″   Welt in Capri   32″ 34″ 36″ 38″ 40″ 42″ 44″

Chart for 'Double Cream'

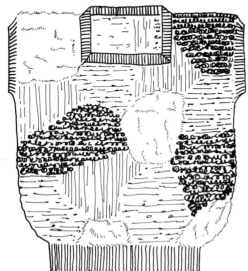

'Double Cream'

Sizes

To fit 32(34,36,38,40,42,44) ins.

Back

Using needles two sizes smaller than those chosen for main tension, e.g. 4 mm (No. 8), and Capri and knitting elastic used together, cast on 85 (89,95,99,105,109,115) sts and work 2 ins in K1,P1 rib, beginning and ending every row K and keeping rib correct in between, and increasing 1 st on the end of the last row on the 2nd, 4th and 6th sizes. (85,90,95,100,105,110,115 sts.)

Break off the knitting elastic and weave in the ends.*

Change to needles chosen for main tension, e.g. 5 mm (No. 6) work the textured areas from the pattern drawing, noting the following points before beginning.

1   Use Dolce single in st.st.
2   Use Capri single in reversed st.st.
3   Use Como single in st.st.
4   Use Pampas double in st.st.
5   On the pattern drawing, the textured areas are given as approximate guides, and need only be roughly followed.
6   A square of graph lines = 1 square inch on this pattern drawing (not a stitch of course!)

Complete the picture so that the work measures $23\frac{1}{2}$ ins from the beginning, ending with a P row.
Next row Cast off 25(27,29,30,32,34,36) sts, K until 25(27,29,30,32,34,36) sts rem., place the 35(36,37,40,41,42,43) sts just worked on to a holder, cast off to end.

Front

Work as for Back as far as *.

Change to larger needles and work the textured areas from the pattern drawing in the same way as for the Back, working until the front is 4 ins shorter than the Back, ending with a P row.

Shape neck Keeping pattern correct as required work next row: Pattern 25(27,29,30,32,34,36) sts turn, and work 4 ins straight on these sts only, ending with a P row.
Cast off.
Place centre 35(36,37,40,41,42,43) sts on to a holder, rejoin yarn to rem. sts, and work 4 ins on these sts also, ending with a P row.
Cast off.

Neckband

Carefully join left shoulder seam.
Using Capri, (without elastic) and smaller needles, pick up and K the 35(36,37,40,41,42,43) sts from the back neck holder, working 2tog. in the centre on the 2nd, 4th and 6th sizes only, pick up and K21 sts down the left front slope, K the first st. from the front neck holder and mark it with a safety pin, K33(34,35,38,39,40,41) sts more from the front holder, working 2tog. in the centre on the 2nd, 4th, and 6th sizes only, K the last st. from the front neck holder and mark it with a safety pin, and K 20 sts up the right neck slope.
Next row (K1,P1) to last 2 sts before marked st., K2tog., P1, K2tog., P1, (K1,P1) to 2 sts before marked st., K2tog., P1, K2tog., (P1,K1) to end.
Next row Rib to 2 sts before the marked st., P2tog., K1, P2tog., rib to 2 sts before the marked st., P2tog., K1, P2tog., rib to end.
Rep. these 2 rows until neck rib measures 1½ ins.
Cast off in rib, decreasing in the same way on this row also.

Armbands

Do not press. Carefully join rem. shoulder seam.
Mark a point at the armhole edge of each piece at each side 8(8½,9,9,9½,9½,10) ins down from the shoulder seam.
Using Capri, (without elastic) and smaller needles, pick up and K, with right side facing, at the rate of 5 sts per inch, 81(85,91,91,95,95,101) sts, and work 8 rows in K1,P1 rib in the same way as before.
Cast off loosely in rib.

Making Up

Do not press. Carefully make up rem. seams.

KNITTING WITH UNUSUAL MATERIALS

Any long flexible filament can be knitted with: gold wire if you can afford it, spaghetti if you have cooked it, hair if you can spare it, or fur if you can face it. More normally, there are lots of odd things that are not yarn, and odd yarns that knit up very well and make exciting fabrics and garments.

Ordinary and fashion yarns are made of all the obvious fibres and mixes: wool, acrylic, cotton, linen, nylon, or more luxuriously, silk, angora, and alpaca. But yarn spinners are now supplying yarns which look like strings and rafias, as well as ribbons and tapes. They are often expensive and a bit overpowering on their own, but look terrific mixed with plainer yarns.

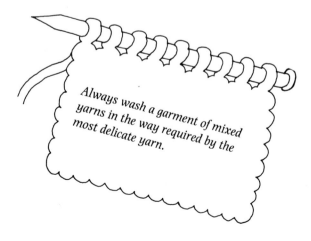

Always wash a garment of mixed yarns in the way required by the most delicate yarn.

Guidance on washing or cleaning these odd yarns is almost always given on the ball band, (see page 132 for further information) but, if in doubt, ask your wool shop, preferably before you buy!

There are lots of other things that knit well and make exciting or funny garments, often cheaply enough for it not to matter if they don't wash or wear very well. Try strips of bias fabric, plastic bags or rags. I have seen lovely bits of knitting done in J-Cloths and bright carrier bags. If the strips are short make a feature of the knots or, to make a much longer, continuous strip, cut spirally from the outside in. More expensively, lengths of chamois leather or even silk knit up spectacularly.

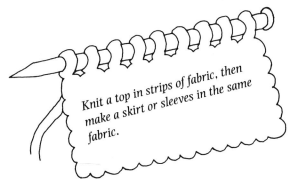

Knit a top in strips of fabric, then make a skirt or sleeves in the same fabric.

You will need to experiment here and play with mixtures and tensions, but these ideas are a great start for youngsters because they are fun, quick and unusual enough to impress their friends.

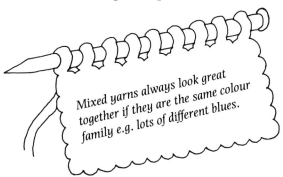

Mixed yarns always look great together if they are the same colour family e.g. lots of different blues.

USING ODD BALLS OF YARN

Any odd balls of yarn that look *good* together can be *used* together. They need to work to similar tensions, but thin ones can always be doubled to achieve this.

If you have odd balls that do not match, tie them into loose skeins and put the whole lot in the same dye bath. They will come out as different versions of the same colour which will then look good together.

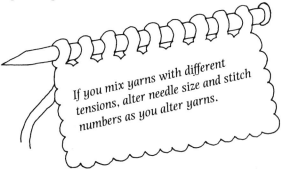

If you mix yarns with different tensions, alter needle size and stitch numbers as you alter yarns.

To discover if you have a sufficient amount of yarn for a jumper, weigh the yarn and then weigh a comparable jumper, or look at a similar pattern to see the amount of yarn you need.

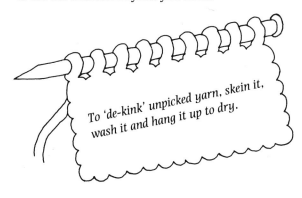

To 'de-kink' unpicked yarn, skein it, wash it and hang it up to dry.

Most yarns can be used again, although some, such as the brushed yarns and bouclés can be difficult to unpick. Take the garment to pieces with great care because indiscriminate chopping means that the unpicked yarn comes away in short, unusable pieces.

'ODD BALL'

This waistcoat uses odd yarns that are easily obtainable in the shops. As well as a basic brushed yarn, there is a silver yarn, and simulated suede strip. It also introduces button and button-hole bands for the first time.

BUTTON BANDS

Traditionally these are worked vertically on a very few stitches and are irritatingly time consuming! It is much easier to use the needles chosen for welts, and look at your tension to discover how many stitches per inch you have. Pick up along the garment edge at this rate and knit the stitches with the right side facing. Then rib until the band is the required width. Cast off in rib. In this way you work a few long rows, much quicker than what feels like thousands of little rows. Do the same for the button-hole band, working the button holes evenly spaced, centrally in the band. On this garment, because it is worked sideways, picking up is unnecessary since you are working in the correct direction already.

To avoid that irritating, untidy loose stitch at one end of a button hole, read on!

Work the row in which stitches are cast off for the button holes, then on the next row, instead of simply casting on the same number of stitches as you cast off, work to one stitch before the button hole, increase one stitch in this stitch, then cast on one less than stated. This increase uses up the loop that makes the button hole untidy, and, of course, by casting on one less you end with the correct number of stitches.

Practise your button holes on this simple garment. I have suggested an arrangement of stripes but you can, of course, do whatever you wish and adjust the size by simply working less or more, before and after the armholes. The waistcoat will be successful as long as both fronts together are approximately the same width as the back.

Choose exciting buttons either as decoration or to close the front opening and, as in the drawing, you can sew buttons decoratively on the band of the turned-back lapel too.

ODD BALL

Materials

Patons Solo Chunky, Black: 8(8,9) × 50 gm balls. Twilleys Double Gold/Silver: 1(1,1) × 100 m reel. Copleys Persuade Grey: 5(5,5) × 25 m skeins. 8 buttons. 1 pr. 6 mm (No. 4) needles. (Or alter to suit your tension if required.)

Tension

15 sts and 19 rows = 4 ins (10 cms) in st.st. on 6 mm (No. 4) needles.

Sizes

To fit up to 34–36(38–40,42–44) ins.
N.B. Where only one figure is given it applies to all sizes.

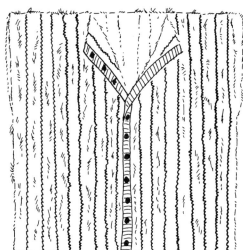

'Odd Ball'

Main Piece (Make one)

Using needles chosen for main tension, e.g. 6 mm (No. 4), and black yarn, cast on 81 sts and work 6 rows in K1,P1 rib beginning and ending every row K and keeping rib correct in between.

Commence stripe pattern:
K8 rows in black yarn.
K2 rows in grey mock suede.
K8 rows in black yarn.
K2 rows in silver.
These 20 rows are repeated throughout.
Work straight until work measures 10(11,12) ins ending with a contrast stripe.
Shape armhole:
*K 3 rows in black yarn, then, keeping pattern correct, cast off 34 sts at beg. of next row, K to end.
Next row K rem. 47 sts.
Cast on 34 sts at beg. of next row. (81 sts)*
Keeping pattern correct (i.e. completing this black stripe, then continuing the pattern), work straight until work measures 20(22,24) ins from the armhole ending with a contrast stripe.
Shape 2nd armhole:
Rep. from * to *.
Keeping pattern correct (i.e. completing this black stripe, then continuing the pattern), work straight until this front matches the first so ending after a complete black stripe.
Rib 2 rows.
Next row Rib 5, (cast off 2, rib 8) to last 6, cast off 2, rib 4.
Rib 2 rows.
Cast off loosely in rib so that the cast-off edge exactly matches the cast-on edge.

Making Up

Do not brush or press. Carefully back stitch shoulder seams together leaving an 8(9,9) ins back neck, and matching all stripes. Stitch on buttons to match button holes.

LACE KNITTING

Knitting lace is very easy. You simply make holes by putting the yarn around the needle, then compensate for this added stitch by knitting two together somewhere else in the pattern. Lace is simply an organised arrangement of these holes.

Don't be put off by the patterns for lace knitting. It is much easier than it looks.

Lace patterns look mind-boggling, the one on page 113 looks as though one needs to struggle through twenty-four rows of pattern, but in fact there are only four rows, arranged in sequence, and even they simply move the pattern across the work. It is just this repetitive symmetry that gives lace its beauty.

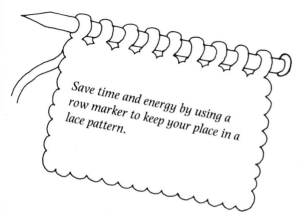

Save time and energy by using a row marker to keep your place in a lace pattern.

You can buy very good plastic row markers that grip the pattern page and even give you a window to show the particular row you're on; or, more simply, use a paper clip or one of those aluminium hair grips, clipped on to the side of your page to keep your place. You will find that you learn the pattern off by heart surprisingly quickly.

Before you begin to knit, go through the pattern and mark your size on each instruction.

If you don't want to mark a favourite book (perhaps even this one!), then make a photocopy and mark that. Most libraries have a photocopier that you can use for a few pence. It really does make life much easier, especially if your pattern has a large number of sizes.

Mark the knitting as well, with safety pins, short lengths of contrast yarn (threaded through or knitted in), paper clips, or the special coloured plastic split rings that are available. These can not only be used to mark shaping and lengths, but also to mark lace pattern repeats at the edges, especially if you are increasing or decreasing and need to find your place to keep the pattern correct.

Look at the lace pattern as you work it and see how it makes the pattern. This makes shaping much easier when you come to it because you can quickly see where you are, especially when you come back to the work after a break, but hopefully you will have marked your pattern too!

Lace was often used for collars and cuffs and

there are some beautiful traditional paterns, some of which have been recently revived (see Bibliography page 139). It may seem tempting to begin lace knitting with these because they are small, but choose with care because some of them are more complicated because of their curved shapes than are the repetitive all-over lace patterns of jumpers.

'LACE'

The especially beautiful lace pattern in the photograph, which has lots of lovely names, such as Frost Flowers, Shooting Star and Pineapple Lace, is much easier than it looks, being basically a four row repeat which moves around to create the alternative pattern.

The jumper has been patterned deliberately simply, with the number of stitches being the number required for the pattern so there are no messy part patterns up the seam, and with straight 'Bishops' sleeves so that no increasings need to be calculated and worked into the pattern.

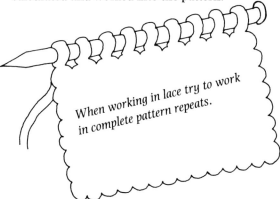

When working in lace try to work in complete pattern repeats.

The only shaping which intrudes into the pattern is the front neck, so take care there, but by then you will know the pattern very well anyway.

Because the pattern is worked in complete lace repeats, the sizes could not be very flexible, as the

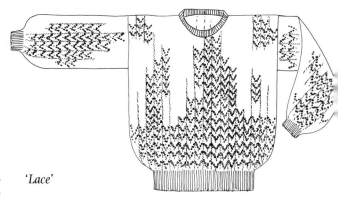

'Lace'

size of the lace governs that of the garment. But the welts are fitting, and the garment is an easy casual style, so choose whichever size gives you plenty of ease.

If you would like to use a more simple lace pattern, like the one in the drawing, then alter the stitch numbers to accommodate the pattern repeat and lose or gain the extra stitches in the shoulder width.

'LACE'

Materials

Wendy Family Choice 4 Ply. Red: 5(6) × 50 gm balls. 1 pr. 3¼ mm (No. 10) needles. 1 pr. 2¾ mm (No. 12) needles. (Or alter to suit your tension if required.)

Tension

28 sts and 36 rows = 4 ins (10 cms) in st.st. on 3¼ mm (No. 10) needles.

Sizes

To fit up to 34 (up to 40) ins.

Back

Using needles two sizes smaller than those chosen for main tension, e.g. 2¾ mm (No. 12), cast on 127(147) sts and work 3 ins in K1,P1 rib, beginning and ending every row K, and keeping rib correct in between.

Next row Rib 3(11), *inc. 1 st. in next st., rib 10(4)*, rep. from * to * to last 3(11), rib to end. (138,172 sts)

Change to Needles chosen for main tension, e.g. 3¼ mm (No. 10) and work in lace pattern:

Row 1 K1, *K3, K2tog., K4, yon, P2, (K2, yon, K2tog.tbl) 3 times, P2, yon, K4, K2tog.tbl., K3*. Rep. from * to * ending K1.

Row 2 K1, *P2, P2tog.tbl., P4, yon, P1, K2, (P2, yon, P2tog.) 3 times, K2, P1, yon, P4, P2tog., P2*. Rep. from * to * ending K1.

Row 3 K1, *K1, K2tog., K4, yon, K2, P2, (K2, yon, K2tog.tbl.) 3 times, P2, K2, yon, K4, K2tog.tbl., K1*. Rep. from * to * ending K1.

Row 4 K1, *P2tog.tbl., P4, yon, P3, K2, (P2, yon, P2tog.) 3 times, K2, P3, yon, P4, P2tog*. Rep. from * to * ending K1.

Row 5 to Row 12 Rep. row 1 to Row 4 twice.

Row 13 K1, *yon, K2tog.tbl., K2, yon, K2tog.tbl., P2, yon, K4, K2tog.tbl., K6, K2tog., K4, yon, P2, K2, yon, K2tog.tbl., K2*. Rep. from * to * ending K1.

Row 14 K1, *yon, P2tog., P2, yon, P2tog., K2, P1, yon, P4, P2tog., P4, P2tog.tbl., P4, yon, P1, K2, P2, yon, P2tog., P2*. Rep. from * to * ending K1.

Row 15 K1, *yon, K2tog.tbl., K2, yon, K2tog.tbl., P2, K2, yon, K4, K2tog.tbl., K2, K2tog., K4, yon, K2, P2, K2, yon, K2tog.tbl., K2*. Rep. from * to * ending K1.

Row 16 K1, *yon, P2tog., P2, yon, P2tog., K2, P3, yon, P4, P2tog., P2tog.tbl., P4, yon, P3, K2, P2, yon, P2tog., P2*. Rep. from * to * ending K1.

Row 17 to Row 24 Rep. Row 13 to Row 16 twice. These 24 rows are repeated throughout the pattern.†

Work straight to a total length of 23 ins ending with a wrong side row which is either the 12th or 24th row of the pattern.

Next row Cast off 44(58) sts, K until 44(58) sts rem., place the 50(56) sts just worked on to a holder, cast off to end.

Front

Work as for Back as far as †, then work straight to a total measurement of 19 ins, so ending with a 12th or 24th, wrong-side row of the pattern. (i.e. 36 rows shorter than the back.)

Shape neck:

Next row Pattern 57(74), turn, P2tog., pattern to end.

**Keeping pattern correct, dec. 1 st. at neck edge on next 5(8) rows, then on every alt. row 8 times. (44,58 sts.)
Work straight until work measures same as Back, and pattern matches that on the Back, so ending with a 12th or 24th row of the pattern.
Cast off.**
Place centre 24 sts on a holder, rejoin yarn to rem. sts, K2tog., pattern to end.
Rep. from ** to **.

Sleeves

Using smaller needles, cast on 69(69) sts and work 3 ins in K1,P1 rib in the same way as for the back.
Next row In rib, inc. 1 st. in every st. (138,138 sts.)
Change to larger needles and lace pattern and work straight to a total measurement of 18(17) ins or desired length to underarm (remembering the amount of ease), ending with 12th or 24th row of pattern.
Cast off loosely.

Neckband

Join left shoulder seam carefully, matching all pattern. Do not press.
With smaller needles and with right side facing, pick up and K the 50(56) sts from the back neck holder, working 2tog. in the middle, 32(36) sts down the left front slope, the 24 sts from the front neck holder, and 32(36) sts up the right neck slope. (137,151 sts.)
Work 14 rows in K1,P1 rib.
Cast off loosely in rib.

Making Up

Carefully join all rem. seams, matching all pattern, and making armholes 10 ins deep. N.B. Grafting is an alternative way of making up delicate fabric. (See page 87.)

PICTURE KNITTING

Once you can colour-knit, (see page 102) the next logical step is to knit pictures, which are great fun, both for the knitter who has the satisfaction of seeing a picture grow, and the wearer who can sport anything from the Pink Panther, to a political statement.

Picture knitting is usually worked from a chart on which each square represents a stitch and is marked in an appropriate colour.

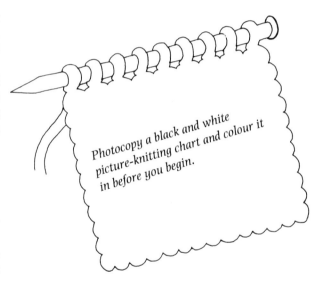

Photocopy a black and white picture-knitting chart and colour it in before you begin.

Charts are usually arranged so that the odd-numbered rows, (first, third, and so on) are knit rows reading from right to left, and so that the purl rows are the even rows and will therefore be worked from left to right. Once you have begun you will recognise bits of the picture easily, and simply relate the row you are working to the row before. Again, it is a good idea to mark your rows in some way to help you to keep your place, (see page 111) even, perhaps, crossing out rows which you have done.

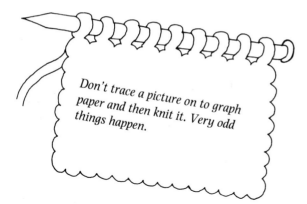

Don't trace a picture on to graph paper and then knit it. Very odd things happen.

MAKING YOUR OWN PICTURE CHARTS

If you want to turn a favourite picture into a knitting chart, you can't simply trace it on to graph paper and then knit the result. This is because knitting stitches are not square, like graph paper squares, and all the pictures will knit up squashed; trees become hedges, houses become bungalows and Great Danes become Dachshunds! So you need to convert the squares of the picture into rectangles of the knitting. Here's how it's done.

1 Measure the space that your knitting is to fill, for example a maximum of about 13 ins wide across a size 24 in jumper, with the maximum picture height being the length of the jumper to the neck, excluding the welt.

2 Square up your chosen picture in one inch squares within these measurements. (*11*)

3 Look at your tension. Typically, a square inch of double knitting is six stitches wide and eight rows high. Mark out the graph paper in the same number of rectangles as there are inch squares marked on your chosen picture. Each rectangle will be six little squares wide and eight little squares high, so representing a knitted square inch.

4 Draw the picture by transferring the lines from one square to the corresponding rectangle on the graph paper (the same way that children do when copying pictures by squaring up). (*12*)

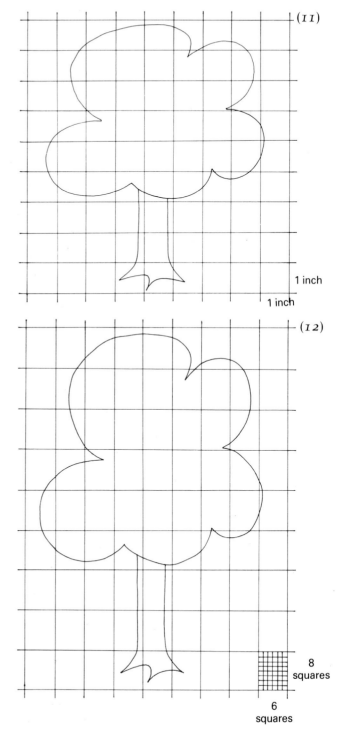

(*11*)

1 inch

1 inch

(*12*)

8 squares

6 squares

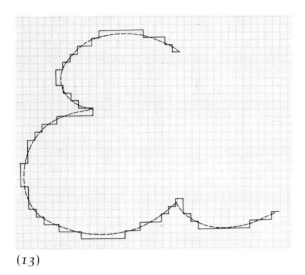

(*13*)

5 Make all the curved lines follow the little
   squares of the graph paper, then fill in your
   colours. (*13*)

When you knit this up, each rectangle from the
graph will become a square inch of knitting and
the picture on the jumper will be just like the original you chose.

   It is possible to get special graph paper for this
job, which saves you all this bother, where the
divisions on the paper are already rectangular, so
a traced drawing will work out exactly like the
original when knitted.

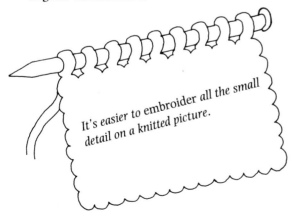

It's easier to embroider all the small detail on a knitted picture.

SURFACE EMBROIDERY

The little fiddly bits of your picture can of course
be embroidered afterwards in just as much detail
and in any stitches you like, and you can add
ribbon curtains, pom-pom trees, appliqué cats, bells,
bows, or whatever you fancy. Remember, though,
that whatever you embroider with must be as
washable as the garment, and the same goes for
any added bits, they need to be washable or easily
removable.

SWISS DARNING

One of the traditional and most attractive ways of
embroidering knitting is Swiss Darning, which
Americans call Duplicate Stitch, a most appropriate name because the embroidery stitch copies and
covers the knitted stitch underneath it.

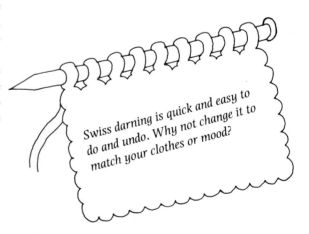

Swiss darning is quick and easy to do and undo. Why not change it to match your clothes or mood?

To Swiss Darn, simply thread a tapestry needle
with contrast thread and come up at the bottom
of a knitted stitch. (*14*)

   Then pass the needle through the stitch above
and down into the same place at the bottom of the
stitch, where the yarn first came from. (*15*)

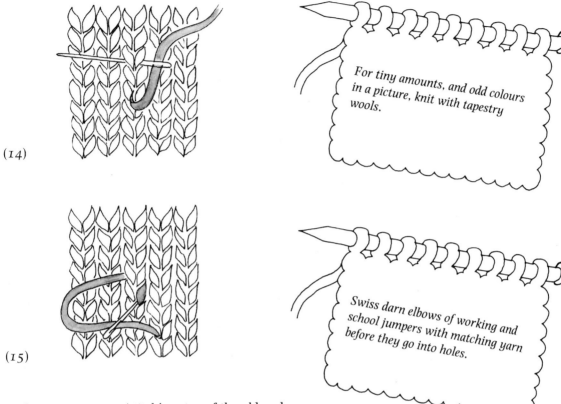

(14)

For tiny amounts, and odd colours in a picture, knit with tapestry wools.

(15)

Swiss darn elbows of working and school jumpers with matching yarn before they go into holes.

This creates a new 'stitch' on top of the old and is easily repeated wherever you like.

It is an ideal technique for fiddly small areas of colour like lettering, and is removable if you change your mind. It is also very quick and can even be worked on bought sweaters so that your teenage daughter can embroider a different pop idol across her front every week, all on the same jumper. So much more versatile than tattoos!

A good idea for Swiss Darning on wool is to use tapestry wools. As well as being available in small amounts, they come in literally hundreds of colours, so for pictures, they give you a choice that knitting wools never can and you won't need to buy a 50 gm ball to knit a bunch of marigolds (orange is an almost impossible colour to buy in knitting yarn).

'OUR HOUSE'

This is a basic double-knitting jumper, with a picture of a house on the front. The chart (pages 120–1) is given for a neat house on the jumper in the photograph, and the drawing shows a slightly more down-at-heel cottage where Cats Rule OK? Why not follow the intructions on page 115 and work out a chart of your own house, knitting different views of it for all the family. Or perhaps your town, a local landmark, Blackpool Tower, The Tower of London, The Leaning Tower of Pisa ... the list of possibilities for picture knitting is literally endless.

Materials

Wendy Family Choice Double Knitting.
Pale blue: 4(4,4,5,5) × 50 gm balls.
Mid green: 2(2,2,2,2) × 50 gm balls.
Dark grey: 2(2,2,2,2) × 50 gm balls.
Brick: 2(2,2,2,2) × 50 gm balls.
Dark green: 1(1,1,1,1) × 50 gm ball.
Small quantities of Pale Grey, White, Red, Dark Brown, Mid Blue, Cream, and Pale Brown. Plus scraps for embroidery.
1 pr. 4 mm (No. 8) needles. 1 pr. 3¼ mm (No. 10) needles. (Or alter to suit your tension if required.)

Tension

24 sts and 32 rows = 4 ins (10 cms) on 4 mm (No. 8) needles over st.st.

Sizes

To fit 32(34,36,38,40) ins.

Back

Work welt and first 8 rows of st.st. in dark grey then work: 2 Rows Pale Brown; 6 rows Pale Grey; 12 rows Mid Green; 15 rows Brick; 1 row Cream; 2 rows of (3 sts Brick, 1 st. Cream); 22 rows Mid Green; 18 rows Dark Green. Complete the rest of the work in Pale Blue.

Using needles two sizes smaller than those chosen for main tension, e.g. 3¼ mm (No. 10), cast on 101(107,111,117,123) sts and work 2½ ins in K1,P1 rib, beginning and ending every row K and keeping rib correct in between.

Change to needles chosen for main tension, e.g. 4 mm (No. 8), and st.st., and work straight until work measures 16 ins ending with a P row.

Shape armholes:

Cast off 5(6,6,6,7) sts at beg. of next 2 rows.

Dec. 1 st. at each end of next 5(5,5,5,5) rows, then every alt. row until 75(77,81,85,89) sts remain.*
Work straight until armholes measure 7(7½,8,8½,9) ins ending with a P row.

'Our House'

Shape shoulders:
Cast off 6(6,6,7,7) sts at beg. of next 6(6,6,6,6) rows, then 5(5,7,5,6) sts at beg. of the foll. 2 rows.
Slip rem. 29(31,31,33,35) sts on to a holder.

Front

Working from the chart, allowing the colours to 'run out' at the sides, and centring up around the centre st.
N.B. The chart is for the smallest size, so you may have more room around your house. Allow clouds to run out at shaping, or move them as you wish. It does not really matter what shape the clouds are.
Work as for Back as far as *, working pattern from chart and keeping chart correct throughout all shapings.
Work straight until armholes measure 4½(5,5,5½,6) ins.
Shape neck:
Work 29(29,31,32,33) sts, turn, and complete this side first.
Dec. 1 st. on neck edge on next 3 rows, then every alt. row until 23(23,25,26,27) sts rem.
Work straight until armholes match those on the Back ending at outside armhole edge.
Shape shoulders:
Cast off 6(6,6,7,7) sts at beg. of next and every alt. row until 5(5,7,5,6) sts rem.
Work 1 row.
Cast off rem. sts.
Slip centre 17(19,19,21,23) sts on to a holder and work other side to match the first.

Right Sleeve

Work in the same colour sequence as for the Back, then 1 in before start of armhole shaping knit in Cloud 'B' so that its left hand edge falls immediately to the right of the centre of the sleeve.
With smaller needles, cast on 47(49,51,53,55) sts and work 24(24,24,28,28) rows in K1,P1 rib in the same way as for the Back.

Change to larger needles and st.st. and inc. 1 st. each end of 7th and every foll. 8th (8th,7th,6th,6th) row until there are 71(75,79,85,89) sts.
Work straight until sleeve measures 18 (18,18,18½,18½) ins, or required length to underarm, ending with a P row.
Shape top:
Cast off 5(6,6,6,7) sts at beg. of the next 2 rows.
Dec. 1 st. at each end of the next 3(3,3,3,3) rows, then every alt. row until 29(27,29,31,31) sts rem.
Dec. 1 st. at each end of the next 5 rows, then cast off 4(3,4,5,5) sts at beg. of the foll. 2 rows.
Cast off rem. 11 sts.

Left Sleeve

Work in the same colour sequence as for the Back, then, at start of armhole shaping knit Cloud 'A' so that its right hand edge falls immediately to the left of the centre of the sleeve.
Work as for Right sleeve.

Neckband

Do not press. Join left shoulder seam.
With smaller needles and Pale Blue, and with right side facing, pick up and knit the sts across the holder at back neck, working 2tog. at centre; 24(24,26,26,28) sts down the left front slope; the sts from front holder; and 24(24,26,26,28) sts up right front slope.
Work 2½(2½,3,3,3) ins in K1,P1 rib in the same way as for the Back welt.
Cast off very loosely in rib.

Making Up

Join all rem. seams using self colours.
Turn neckband on to wrong side and loosely slip st. down.
Embroider any detail you wish.

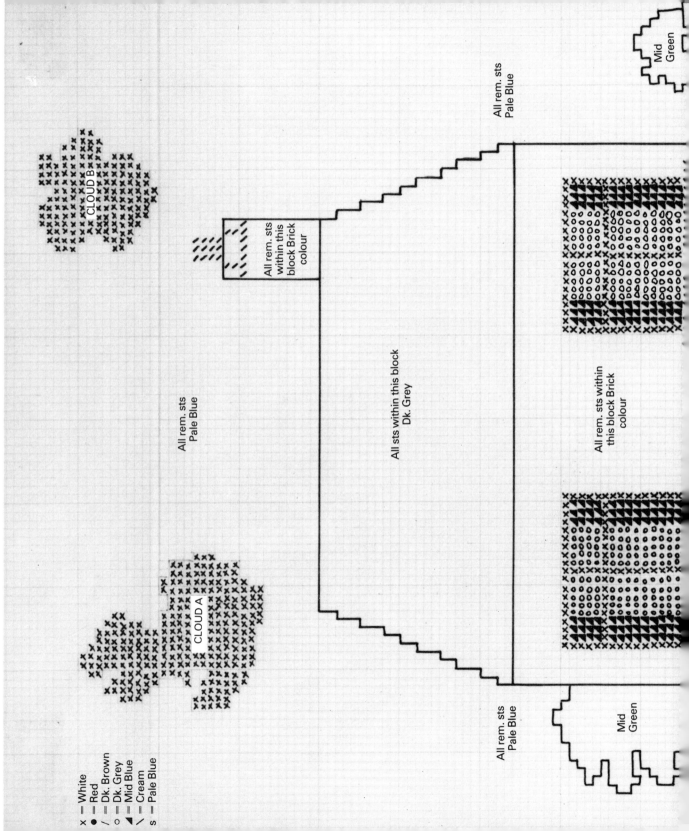

CLOUD B

CLOUD A

All rem. sts
Pale Blue

All rem. sts within this block Brick colour

All sts within this block
Dk. Grey

All rem. sts within
this block Brick
colour

All rem. sts
Pale Blue

All rem. sts
Pale Blue

Mid
Green

Mid
Green

x = White
● = Red
/ = Dk. Brown
o = Dk. Grey
◣ = Mid Blue
╱ = Cream
s = Pale Blue

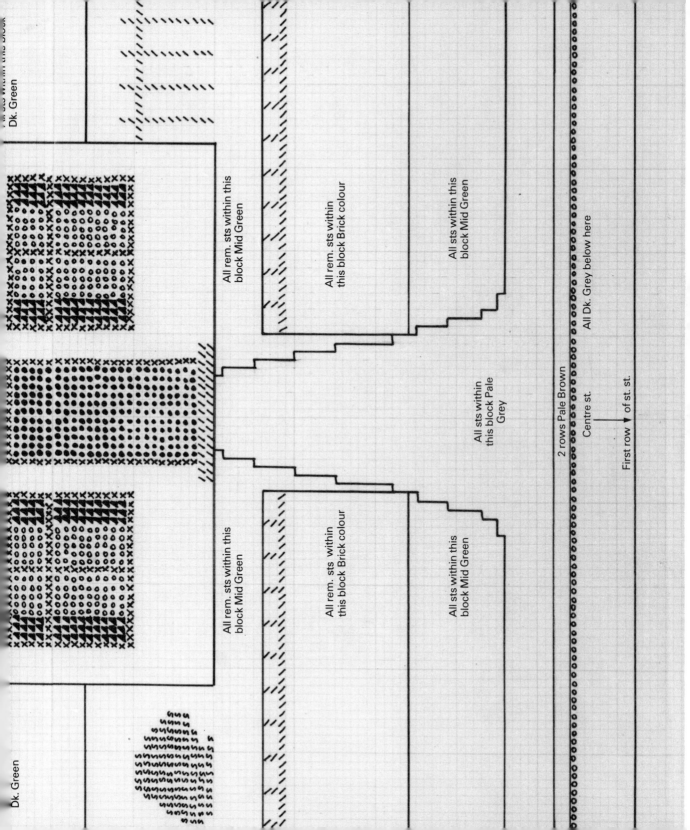

Dk. Green

Dk. Green

All rem. sts within this block Mid Green

All rem. sts within this block Brick colour

All sts within this block Mid Green

All rem. sts within this block Mid Green

All rem. sts within this block Brick colour

All sts within this block Pale Grey

All sts within this block Mid Green

2 rows Pale Brown

Centre st.

All Dk. Grey below here

First row ▶ of st. st.

FAIR ISLE KNITTING

If you have been working through the techniques in this book, you should have colour knitting 'all stitched up' by now, having done random colour blocks on the jumper on page 104, and picture knitting from page 114. However, one technique remains in colour knitting that has traditionally provided us with some of the loveliest patterns, and that is Fair Isle.

The knitters of Fair Isle work ridiculously fast, in the round, usually only two colours at a time although these may change as the work progresses. In Fair Isle, unlike picture knitting, the yarns are loosely stranded across the back because the two yarns will be used alternately across the work. Never pull the yarns tight, but allow them to lie in place. If a yarn is crossing more than two or three stitches it should be woven in by placing it behind the working yarn as shown. (16)

If bands of Fair Isle pull your work in, use larger needles for these rows only.

When working across a row of Fair Isle knitting, always pick one yarn up under the other, and the second yarn always over. In this way you prevent the yarns from twisting, as the crossing of the yarns for one colour is cancelled out by crossing them the other way for the next.

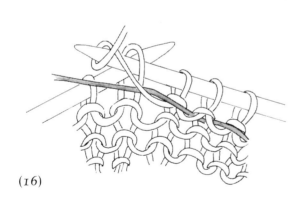

(16)

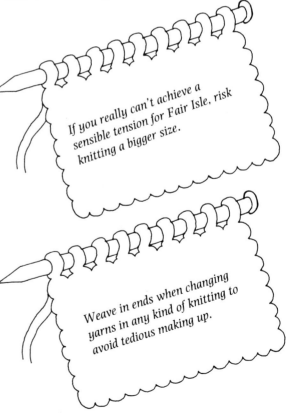

If you really can't achieve a sensible tension for Fair Isle, risk knitting a bigger size.

Weave in ends when changing yarns in any kind of knitting to avoid tedious making up.

This weaving in prevents loops of yarn on the back which look ugly and catch, and it can also give a neater, firmer fabric.

Watch your tension with Fair Isle! It almost always pulls work in, so use bigger needles and, if work is in an all-over Fair Isle pattern, work your tension square in the pattern too.

Many of the Fair Isle traditional patterns are inspired by the sea or by folk lore, and there are some beautiful ones in varying degrees of complexity, for you to copy and experiment with. For some sources of these patterns see the Bibliography on page 139. Many of these patterns, too, incorporate the decorative decreasing which is such a feature of Fair Isle jumper yokes and Tam-o'-shanters.

'BRIGHT'

This pattern simplifies a traditional Fair Isle stitch pattern, and uses it in modern bright colours all over a plain cream jacket. Remember how important tension is over an all-over Fair Isle pattern. Choose sizes with care on a Fair Isle garment because the fabric does not stretch like plain knitting.

Materials

Patons Cotton Soft in Cream. 8(8,9,9) × 50 gm balls, and 1(2,2,2) × 50 gm balls of each of: Pink, Orange, Yellow, Green and Blue. 1 pr. 4 mm (No. 8) needles. 1 pr. 3¾ mm (No. 9) needles. (Or alter to suit your tension if required.)

Tension

24 sts and 28 rows = 4 ins (10 cms) on 4 mm (No. 8) needles in st.st. over pattern.

Sizes

To fit 32–34(36–38,40–42,44–46) ins. Actual 37(41,45,49) ins.

Back

Using needles one size smaller than those chosen for main tension, e.g. 3¾ mm (No. 9), cast on (in Cream) 111(123,135,147) sts and work 6 rows in st.st. starting P.

Next row (Hemline): K.
Change to needles chosen for main tension, e.g. 4 mm (No. 8), and cont. in st.st. starting K, and work straight in pattern as follows:

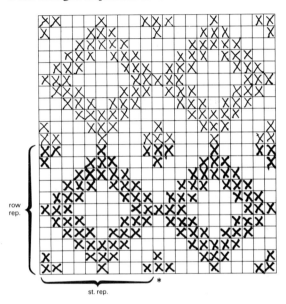

row
rep.

st. rep.

On the chart the stitch marked * = 1st (2nd,3rd,4th) st. of first K row after hemline, so work establishing row then keep pattern correct; the background is always cream. The other colours are used as contrasts, changing after each 11-row repeat in the following order.
1st contrast pink
2nd contrast orange
3rd contrast yellow
4th contrast green
5th contrast blue
Repeat this sequence throughout.
Work straight in this colour sequence to a total measurement of 23 ins ending with a P row and as near as possible after a complete repeat.
Cast off 32(37,41,46) sts K until 32(37,41,46) sts rem., cast off to end.
Place the 47(49,53,55) sts at the centre back on to a holder.

Left Front

Using smaller needles and Cream, cast on 55 (61,67,73) sts and work 6 rows of st.st. starting P.
Next row (Hemline): K.
Change to larger needles and cont. in st.st. in pattern and colour sequence as for Back starting K, but on the first pattern row, the st. marked * is the 5th(1st,7th,3rd) st. of the first K row after the hemline, then the pattern is kept correct throughout, and should finish at the left hand edge after a complete repeat.
Work straight until Front is 32 rows shorter than the Back, so ending with a P row.†
**Next row* (to shape neck): Keeping pattern and colour sequence correct, work 43(49,54,59) sts, turn, and leave rem. 12(12,13,14) sts on a holder.
Dec. 1 st. at neck edge on next 6(6,7,7) rows, then every alt. row until 32(37,41,46) sts. rem.
Work 15(13,12,12) rows straight (so that Front is now the same length as Back to armhole edge).
Cast off.

Right Front

Work as for Left Front as far as † in pattern and colour sequence. On all sizes the stitch marked * is the first st. of the first K row after the hemline, and the pattern is allowed to run out at the armhole edge, so matching the front opening edges.
After † work:
Next row K.
Work as for Left Front from ** to end, working one row less straight before casting off.

Sleeves

Using smaller needles and Cream, cast on 61 sts and work 6 rows in st.st. starting P.
Next row (Hemline): K. Change to larger needles.
Continue in st.st. starting K, in colour and pattern sequence as given for Back, (the st. marked * is the

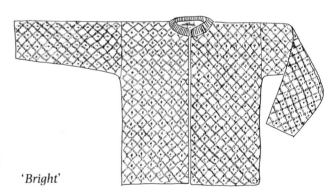

'*Bright*'

first st. of this first K row on every size), and, keeping pattern correct, working all increases into the pattern, inc. 1st. each end of every 4th(3rd,3rd,3rd) row until there are 103 (115,115,121) sts.

Work straight to a total measurement of 18½ ins ending with a P row, and as near as possible after a complete repeat.

Cast off loosely.

Making Up, Bands and Facings

Do not press or brush.
Join both shoulder seams.

Neckband

Using smaller needles, and with right side facing, pick up and K 12(12,13,14) sts from holder at right front neck; 34(34,36,38) sts up right front slope; 47(49,53,55) sts from back neck holder; 33(35,35,37) sts down Left Front slope, and 12(12,13,14) sts from left front holder. (138, 142,150,158 sts.)
Commence rib:
Row 1 K2, (P2,K2) to end.
Row 2 P2, (K2,P2) to end.
Rep. these 2 rib rows 4 more times.
K1 row.
Beg. with Row 2, work 10 more rib rows.
Cast off in rib.

Folding the neckband along the K row, turn it on to the wrong side and loosely slip st. down.
Mark a point each side, back and front, on the edges, 8½(9½,9½,10) ins. down from the shoulder seam. Seam sides up to this point, so making 8½(9½,9½,10) in deep armholes. Turn bottom hem up on to wrong side and loosely slip st. down.

Front Facings (Both alike)

Using larger needles and with right side facing,

pick up and K, at the rate of 6 sts per inch, 100 sts up the Front edge from a point immediately above the hem, to the top of the main Front piece, excluding neckband.
K1 row.
Work 6 rows in st.st. starting K.
Cast off loosely.
Turn these facings on to the wrong side and loosely slip st. down.
Seam and insert sleeves, turn sleeve hem on to wrong side and loosely slip st. down.

HEMS AND FACINGS

The 'Bright' jumper had hems and facings worked to turn back on to the wrong side, instead of welts and bands. You have to do something to neaten the edges of stocking stitch or they will roll, and hems look good. When you have picked up along the edge, at the rate of stitches per inch of your tension, work one reversed row, e.g. a knit row with the wrong side facing you. Then work your hem in stocking stitch. This reversed row gives a neat sharp edge rather than a rolled turn.

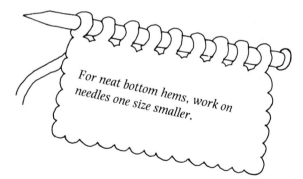

For neat bottom hems, work on needles one size smaller.

Because knitting folds thickly, it is necessary to mitre the corner of these hems if they meet, to avoid a treble thickness of knitting. To do this, simply decrease one stitch at each end of every row throughout the working of the facing or hem.

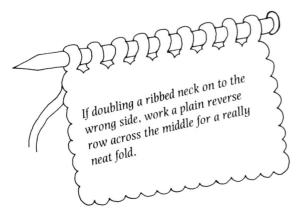

If doubling a ribbed neck on to the wrong side, work a plain reverse row across the middle for a really neat fold.

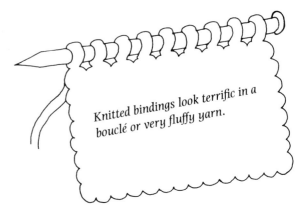

Knitted bindings look terrific in a bouclé or very fluffy yarn.

BINDING

Knitting can also be bound at the edges, with fabric if you wish, but more satisfactorily and sympathetically with knitting. Pick up along the edge of the knitting and work a few rows of reversed stocking stitch, which rolls the right way. Then cast off and catch down the binding all along.

Knitted-in bindings behave better if caught down on the right side.

Or knit a separate strip of reversed stocking stitch, either longways or width ways and attach it afterwards. Bindings need not of course be the same yarn or tension as the main fabric, and look particularly good in contrast colours or in plain yarns when the main garment is textured.

WORKING IN THE ROUND

Working in the round instead of backwards and forwards, is a traditional technique with many advantages. Indeed it is really the obvious thing to do in a craft like knitting where the garment and fabric are made at the same time from one continuous thread. Many traditional patterns were worked in this way, and indeed still are, and one of the reasons for dividing garments into pieces is that when patterns began to be written down rather than passed on by word of mouth, it was easier to write them down if the garments were split up in the way that we now accept.

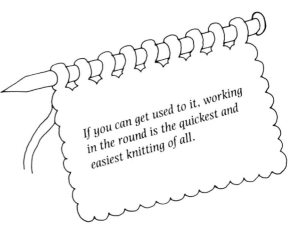

If you can get used to it, working in the round is the quickest and easiest knitting of all.

When working in the round, you begin at the welt and make a tube as far as the beginning of the armhole. Then, you can either work the front yoke and back yoke separately, cast the shoulders off together, work the neck, and then pick up around the armholes and work to the cuff; or you can work each sleeve to armhole level too, and then pick up around the entire garment and work a circular yoke. There are several advantages in this technique:

There is no making up to do when the knitting is complete.

It is quicker because the work is not constantly being reversed.

To work stocking stitch you work in knit all the time, which is quicker and easier. (You do, really. Think about it!)

The right side of the work always faces you. This is a great advantage in colour knitting and Fair Isle, as you can see what you are doing all the time.

Obviously, you will need to work on double-ended or circular needles, and which of these you choose is purely a personal preference. Double-ended needles are very versatile and can cope with any number of stitches, but you need to move from one needle to another, and some people find all the ends bothersome, if not painful!

Spread a large number of stitches across several double ended needles, or a circular needle, even if you are not working in the round.

Circular needles are also very versatile and you can work in both directions on a very large number of stitches if you wish. When working in the round you need varying lengths, as well as sizes, of circular needle, because, for example, a needle long enough to go around the body of a garment will be too long for the number of stitches in a cuff welt.

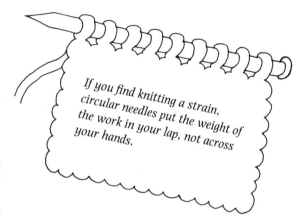

If you find knitting a strain, circular needles put the weight of the work in your lap, not across your hands.

If you tend to get lost in circular knitting, mark the beginning of the rounds or the armhole positions with stitch markers.

Traditional Guernsey knitters work a mock seam of reversed stitches up the sides of garments in order to keep their place. As with Aran and Fair Isle knitting, there is a wealth of traditional Guernsey, or Gansey knitting in a custom that is still alive today, when fishermen still have knitted, or knit, totally personal fishing 'shirts'. (See the Bibliography on page 139 for collections of these fascinating patterns.)

WORKING TWO CAST-OFF EDGES TOGETHER

The shoulder seams of any garment can be cast off together to give a neat, flat join which is much more satisfying than a bulky seam. This can also be worked decoratively on the right side, perhaps even in a contrast yarn. (For the technique, see the making-up instructions in the following pattern.) Casting off two shoulder edges together works even when the shoulders are stepped in the conventional way. Simply turn and leave the worked groups of stitches on the needle instead of casting them off. Then cast both shoulders off together as before.

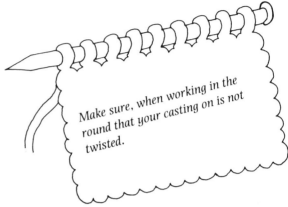

Make sure, when working in the round that your casting on is not twisted.

For a neat and stretchy professional finish, cast off shoulders together.

'FISHERMAN'

This garment uses all these techniques of working in the round, and so has no making up at all. It is much more simple than the traditional Guernsey in the drawing, being a basic garment in a natural colour, and, if you have never worked in the round before, here is the easy place to begin.

Be careful to start with! Be very sure that your casting on is not twisted around the needles when you begin your first round. Traditionally the welt was halved and each was worked separately on a pair of needles. The first round was then worked across both welt tops. If you get in a pickle with casting on in the round, you could try this.

N.B. The measurement worked at *** will give an underarm seam length of $18(18\frac{1}{2},18\frac{1}{2},19,19)$ ins. If you wish to vary this, then make the alteration at ***, before the sleeve shaping begins.

Materials

Patons Capstan Aran Cream $14(14,15,15,16)\times$ 50gm balls.
$3\frac{1}{2}$ mm (No. 9) circular needle – long and short.
4 mm (No. 8) circular needle – short.
$4\frac{1}{2}$ mm (No. 7) circular needle – long and short.
5 mm (No. 6) circular needle – short.
Or sets of double-ended needles. (Or alter sizes to suit your tension if required.)

Tension

19 sts and 25 rows = 4 ins (10 cms) on $4\frac{1}{2}$ mm (No. 7) needles in st.st.

Sizes

To fit $36(38,40,42,44)$ ins.

Main Piece

Using a circular needle, or set of double-ended needles, two sizes smaller than those chosen for main tension, e.g. 3½mm (No 9), cast on 180(188,200,208,220) sts and work in rounds of K2,P2 rib until work measures 2 ins taking care to end after a complete round.

Mark this point in the round with a pin. (or piece of contrast yarn or a stitch marker.)

Change to a needle, or needles chosen for main tension, e.g. 4½mm (No. 7), and work in K rounds, (i.e. st.st.) until work measures a total of 14½(14½,15,15,15½) ins, ending after a complete round.

Divide for armholes and work Back:

K90(94,100,104,110) sts, turn and P back.

Work straight in st.st (on two needles if you wish) until armholes measure 8½(9,9,9,9½) ins (work measures 23,23½,24,24,25 ins) ending with a P row.

Leave these sts on a spare needle or holder.

Work Front:

Rejoin yarn to rem. 90(94,100,104,110) sts and work in st.st until work is 20 rows shorter than the back, so ending with a P row.

Shape neck:

Next row K35(36,39,40,42) sts, turn, P2tog.tbl., P to end.

**Keeping armhole edge straight, dec. 1 st. at neck edge on next 3 rows, then on every alt. row until 27(28,31,32,34) sts rem.

Work straight until armhole measures same as on the Back, (i.e. work 7 rows straight so ending at armhole edge with a P row.)**

Join left shoulder:

Turn the work inside out and, with the wrong side of the front facing, place Front and Back left shoulder top edges together, each on a spare needle.

Using a spare needle of the same size, pick up 1 st. from the outside edge of the Front shoulder and 1 st. from the Back. K them together. K together the 2nd st. from each needle in the same way and pass the first st. over.

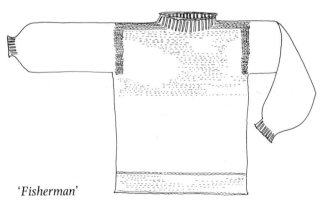

'Fisherman'

Continue in this way until 26(27,30,31,33) pairs of sts have been cast off. fasten off the 27th(28th,31st,32nd,34th)st. (63,66,69,72,76 sts rem. on the Back.)

Turn the work the right way out again.

Rejoin yarn to inside of rem. sts of the Front, K20(22,22,24,26) sts and place them on a holder, K to end.

Next row P to last 2, P2tog.

Rep. from ** to **.

Join right shoulder seam:

Turn the work inside out and, with the wrong side of the Back facing, cast off the two top shoulder edges in the same way as before until no sts rem. on the Front top shoulder edge.

Slip the stitch remaining from the casting off on to a pin. Do not break off yarn.

Turn the work the right way out again.

With a 3¾ mm (No. 9) short circular needle, and with right side facing, pick up and K the stitch from the pin, 36(38,38,40,42) sts still remaining at the Back neck, working 2tog. in the middle, 16 sts down the left Front slope, the 20(22,22,24,26) sts from the Front neck holder, and 16 sts up the right neck slope. (88,92,92,96,100 sts.)

Work in rounds of K2,P2 rib for 1 in.

Change to a needle one size larger and work to a total of 2 ins of rib.

Change to 4½ mm (No. 7) needles and work to a total of 4 ins of rib.

Change to a needle one size larger still (i.e. 5 mm) and work to a total of 6 ins of rib.

Cast off loosely in rib.

Sleeves (Both alike)

With a 4½ mm (No. 7) short circular, or 4 double-ended needles, beginning at the bottom of the armhole opening, with right side facing, pick up and K40(42,42,42,46) sts up one side of the armhole, and 40(42,42,42,46) sts down the other. (80,84,84,84,92 sts.)

Work in st.st. (i.e. every round K) until sleeve measures 4(6½,6½,7,5) ins *** ending after a complete round, i.e. at armhole bottom.

Next round: K2tog.tbl. K to last 3, K2tog., K1. K3(2,2,2,2) rounds.

Repeat the last 4(3,3,3,3) rounds until there are 44 sts, finishing with the 3(2,2,2,2) plain rounds. Change to a 3¾ mm (No. 9) needle or needles and work 2½ ins in rounds of K2,P2 rib.

Cast off loosely in rib.

Do not press. There is no making up.

SHAPING WITH NEEDLE SIZE

As I mentioned when talking about Fair Isle, you can use needle size to correct the way in which stitch patterns alter the tension of your knitting. You can also use needle size to make a plain fabric do what you want it to do.

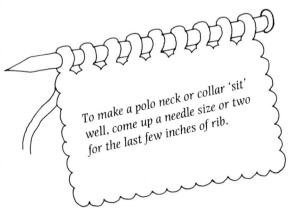

To make a polo neck or collar 'sit' well, come up a needle size or two for the last few inches of rib.

Just as larger needles will ease tight casting off, so they will ease a fabric out to make it spread. So, with things like polo necks and collars, work your way steadily up through the needle sizes for a super fit. It is much easier than increasing within rib, and looks much neater because it does not alter the stitch numbers. This technique of altering needle sizes also works beautifully for cowl necks, which can be tightened up again on to smaller needles at the end to give the soft draped effect in the middle.

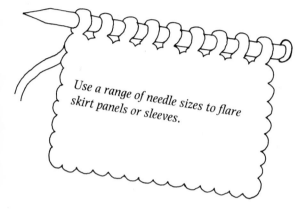

Use a range of needle sizes to flare skirt panels or sleeves.

WASHING

When washing knitwear, follow the yarn ball-band instructions whenever possible and, if in doubt, go gently.

Don't throw all your ball bands away before you have checked washing instructions.

WASHING SYMBOLS

If washing symbols on ball bands look all Greek to you, there's a list on page 132 to help you read the runes. If in doubt, ask, either your wool shop or dry cleaners. When washing by hand, a special wool shampoo is preferable, as soap powders can be difficult to dissolve and any undissolved bits affect the yarn. Avoid detergents and too much heat, and avoid picking the garment out of the water when it is full of water, as the weight will pull it out of shape.

Tougher garments can be spun dried, but if in doubt, squeeze out the excess water and roll the garment flat in a towel.

Don't tumble dry hand knits. It's far too drastic.

Dry flat if at all possible, it's surprising how much quicker they do dry, and avoid tumble drying unless you are sure it's safe. I have seen a beautiful designer sweater reduced to a string vest and bag of fluff by tumble drying!

Dry away from direct sunlight. It can affect colours, especially in wool.

WASHING SYMBOLS

 1. Can be washed. Number above line refers to number on machine, number below is water temperature in centigrade for hand or machine.

 2. Wash by hand only.

 3. Do not wash.

 4. Can be dry cleaned.

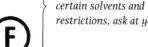 *5, 6, 7 & 8. Can only be dry cleaned in certain solvents and with certain restrictions, ask at your dry cleaners.*

 9. Do not dry clean.

 10. Tumble dries well.

 11. Do not tumble dry.

 12. And 'C1' = can be bleached with chlorine. If crossed out, do not bleach.

 13. Iron up to 210°C (hot).

 14. Iron up to 160°C (warm).

 15. Iron up to 120°C (cool).

 16. Do not iron or press in any way.

If all this seems a ridiculous fuss, then choose yarns that can take the tough life, especially for children, and throw them in the washing machine and out on to the line to take their chances. Many modern yarns can stand this treatment. It just needs careful choosing in the first place.

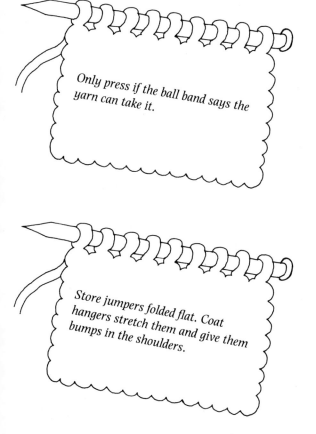

Only press if the ball band says the yarn can take it.

Store jumpers folded flat. Coat hangers stretch them and give them bumps in the shoulders.

ALTERING EXISTING GARMENTS

If, in spite of all your efforts, your knitted garments do not fit the person they were intended for, or that person grows, puts on weight or wants to alter the style, here are some ways of making the changes without having to start all over again.

Too Short?

Using a small circular needle, pick up every stitch of the first row of stocking stitch above the welt all around the garment. Cut off the welt, (go on, be brave!) and then knit a contrast or matching stripe of stocking stitch and a new welt, adding the extra length you want. Cast off loosely so that the garment is still easy to get on.

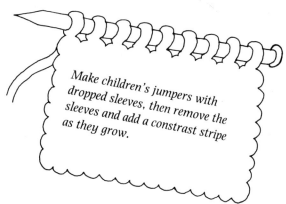

Make children's jumpers with dropped sleeves, then remove the sleeves and add a constrast stripe as they grow.

Too Long?

Use the same techniques as for lengthening, but pick up around the stocking stitch well above the welt, removing as much as you want to. Cut it all off and knit only a new welt. It is not possible to loose the cuff end of a sleeve in this way as it will be too wide further up, so remove sleeves, undo the top back to the straight section and remove extra length before re-making the top.

Too Big?

Give it away or wait for someone to grow into it! Because this is the most difficult alteration to make. The best way is to undo all of the seams and then, using a sewing machine, run a double line of machining all around the edge where you would like the garment pieces to end, then cut off all the surplus outside the machining and re-make the garment. This technique, called cut and sew, sounds and is rather drastic, but it does work so long as the knitting isn't too bulky, soft or lacy to machine properly.

Too Small?

Undo the side seams and add decorative pieces up the sides. Or cut and sew (see previous section) straight down the centre front and add wide button bands or a contrast stripe. A stripe could be worked up the back too.

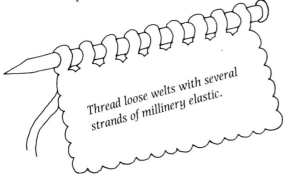

Thread loose welts with several strands of millinery elastic.

the number to share it between the back and the front, then simply add this number to the number of stitches cast on. When you come to the shaping, leave the armhole and neck shaping the same, as these vary very little anyway, and divide the additional stitches between the two shoulders, adding them to the shaping all through and then casting them off evenly across the shoulder top.

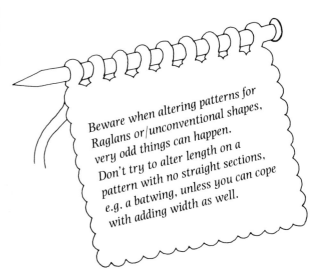

Beware when altering patterns for Raglans or/unconventional shapes, very odd things can happen. Don't try to alter length on a pattern with no straight sections, e.g. a batwing, unless you can cope with adding width as well.

ALTERING PATTERNS

Length

This is easy, and most of us do this automatically. Simply work more or less in the straight part of the piece of work you are knitting.

Size

If you would like to alter a pattern to your chosen size before you start to knit then simply look at the tension and work out how many stitches there are to the inch, decide by how many inches you would like to alter the pattern, and so work out the number of stitches you need to add or remove. Halve

TEACHING PEOPLE TO KNIT

If you can teach someone to knit and catch their enthusiasm, you have given them a hobby of great satisfaction which will last them for life. This book begins with the simplest garment of all, so read the first section beginning on page 76 then take a beginner into the 'drooliest' wool shop you can find and help with the choice of an irresistible yarn and start them on their first garment.

Just to help, here are a few ideas:

1 Do cast on for a learner, it is a different tech-

nique from actual knitting and much easier to learn when you can already knit.

2 Knit the first few rows for them, they are always the most difficult.

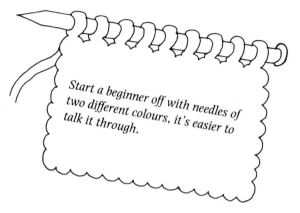

Start a beginner off with needles of two different colours, it's easier to talk it through.

3 Sit the new knitter next to you and knit as well, so that they copy what you do. Take it very slowly stage by stage, and be prepared to repeat and correct all the time.

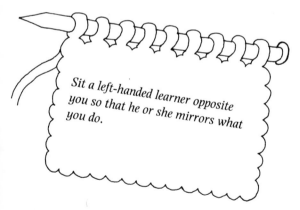

Sit a left-handed learner opposite you so that he or she mirrors what you do.

4 Make sure that each old stitch is removed, if not the knitting gets bigger and bigger all the time! And catch dropped stitches early, before they do too much damage.

5 Perhaps most important of all, achieve something, whatever it is! Start children off on finger puppets and little toys so that they quickly have a result they can be proud of. (See Bibliography for ideas, page 139.)

MAKING KNITTED TOYS

Knitted toys are lovely and loveable. They are squashy and floppy, washable and good to sleep with, and, if the worst comes to the worst, and number one favourite toy is lost on the bus, you can make it again exactly the same.

As with anything else for small children, safety is of first importance, so check all of your materials. Yarns should not be too fluffy, eyes and noses should be of a safe kind that do not detach and are completely safe. Stuffing should be non-toxic and any trimmings should be very firmly stitched on.

Make sure that everything is washable too, it is worth investing in proper washable toy stuffing as many home-made stuffings are heavy or lumpy or wash badly. If you have enough patience, and bits, the left-over bits of yarn from making up other garments are good for stuffing small toys.

Take great care and time with toys' faces, they make all the difference.

KNITTED SOFT FURNISHINGS

Traditionally, some of the most exquisite knitting is the lace table cloth and mat knitting. Particularly from Central Europe, especially Vienna. For the dedicated knitter, there are patterns available for these, and, for the less ambitious among us, there are patterns for modern lace table cloths and even curtains, if you have the stamina!

The easiest furnishing to make though is the cushion. Knit a picture (or a texture, or a super yarn) into a square, back it, or make two, stuff, and it's finished. Cushion making is quite compulsive. Try out lots of stitch patterns and techniques on equal-sized squares in the same yarn, like a sampler, and make a patchwork cushion. Try out that elaborate technique you really can't face knitting over a garment, and make a cushion square instead.

Get everyone in the office to knit one counterpane square and make a cot quilt or bedspread as a lovely leaving or retiring present.

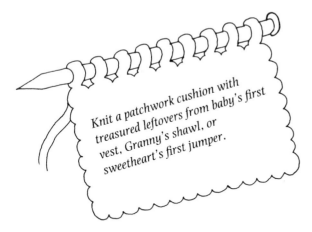

Knit a patchwork cushion with treasured leftovers from baby's first vest, Granny's shawl, or sweetheart's first jumper.

The knitting of counterpane squares in traditional patterns has always been done, and the resulting bedspreads are heirlooms, expensive in time, of course, but cheap in materials.

KNITTING FOR THE DISABLED

Knitting is wonderful therapy. Ever since the Shetland shawls were knitted by the ailing lassies who were too unwell to work gutting fish and cutting turfs, and so had soft-enough hands to cope with the finest yarn, knitting has been a constructive time-filler, comfort and satisfying creative craft for people who are confined to bed or armchair, or who have other handicaps.

If your husband 'can't get about like he used to', get him knitting in front of Match of the Day!

Apart from the light needles and circular needles mentioned before on page 77, there are gadgets to help people with only the use of one hand, knitting frames designed for one hand, talking patterns for the blind, and special yarns for those allergic to wools. For a list of addresses where information can be obtained about these see page 138.

Children with poor sight love the feel of knitted toys. Try it!

APPENDIX

For further information on yarn stockists, contact:

Wendy Wools
Carter & Parker Ltd
Gordon Mills
Guiseley
West Yorkshire
LS20 9PD.

Patons & Baldwins Ltd
PO Box
Darlington
Co. Durham DL1 1YQ

For stockists of additional materials, trims and accessories, contact:

H.G. Twilley Ltd
Roman Mill
Stamford
Lincolnshire PE9 1BG

L. Copley Smith & Sons
PO Box
Darlington
Co. Durham DL1 1YW

Welsh Products Ltd
(Glamor)
Goatmill Road
Dowlais
Merthyr Tydfil
Mid Glamorgan
CF48 3TE

Henry Millward & Sons
Ltd
Studley
Warwickshire B80 7AS

Useful Addresses
The following will gladly supply details upon receipt of a stamped addresed envelope.

For resources for teachers of knitting crafts:

The Knitting Craft Group
PO Box 6
Thirsk
North Yorkshire YO7 1TA

For knitting chart design graph paper:

Tricot Products
Parsonage Hill
Somerton
Somerset TA11 7PF

For specialist Shetland yarns and materials:

Jamieson & Smith (SWB) Ltd
90 North Road
Lerwick
Shetland Isles ZE1 0PQ

For information on 'talking' knitting patterns:

RNIB
224 Great Portland Street
London W1N 6AA

Knitting for allergy sufferers:

Cotton On
29 North Clifton Street
Lytham FY8 5HW

For one-handed knitting:

Knitterella Ltd
21 Kingsland High Street
London E8

or for any enquiries about knitting for the disabled contact your local DHSS or:

Disabled Living Foundation
380–384 Harrow Road
London W9 2HU

BIBLIOGRAPHY

For stitch patterns and ideas:

The Harmony Guide to Knitting Stitches (Lyric, 1983)

Mary Thomas's Book of Knitting Patterns (Hodder & Stoughton, 1943)

Vogue Dictionary of Knitting Stitches Anne Matthews (David & Charles, 1984)

For Traditional Knitting patterns:

The Art of Knitting Eve Harlow (Collins, 1977)

The Complete Book of Traditional Knitting Rae Compton (Batsford, 1983)

Heritage on Knitting Series of Traditional Lace Patterns Tessa Lorant (Thorn Press, 1981–4)

Traditional Knitting Michael Pearson (Collins, 1984)

Traditional Knitting in the British Isles Gwyn Morgan (Ward Lock, 1981)

INDEX: KNITTING